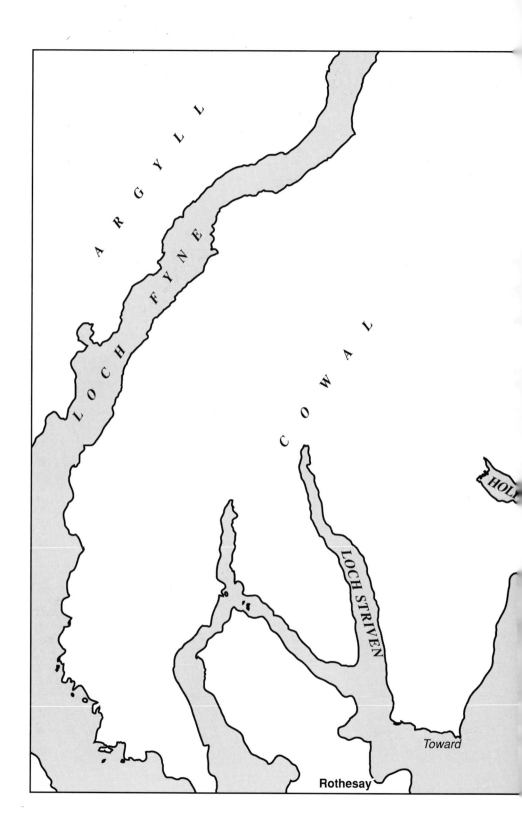

LOCH
LONG

Finnart

Garelochhead

Faslane

Glen Fruin

pipe line

LOCH
LOMOND

Drymen

oulpor

Peaton
Hill

Clynder

Stroul

Rhu

Rosneath

Camsail

Helensburgh

Craigendoran

Balloch

ove

Portkil

GARE LOCH

Kilcreggan

River Leven

GOUROCK

GREENOCK

DUMBARTON

PORT GLASGOW

Bowling

Old
Kilpatrick

R E N F R E W S H I R E

United States Navy Base Two

AMERICANS AT ROSNEATH 1941–45

Dennis Royal

The Douglas Press

First published 2000 by
The Douglas Press
1 Duiletter
Glendaruel
Colintraive
Argyll
PA22 3AE
fax: 01369 820372

ISBN 1 902831 80 2

Printed by
Cordfall Ltd
0141 572 0878

CONTENTS

PHOTOGRAPHIC SOURCES

Imperial War Museum: pages 14, 16, 84, 85.
British Crown Copyright / MOD Reproduced with the permission of HMSO: pages 89, 90.
US National Archives: pages 28, 32 (top), 34, 39, 46, 47, 48, 54, 56, 59, 60, 62, 64, 66, 67, 76.
US Navy Navfac Archives: pages 29, 30, 33 (top).
USN Submarine Force Museum: page 57.
James Hall Collection. Reproduced by permission of Mr N. Burniston: page 35.
Ted Humes's Collection: pages 32 (lower), 33 (lower), 36, 53, 57.
Patricia Drayton: pages 61, 86.
Tom Fulton: page 24.
Mrs R. McMorran: page 13.
Mrs S. Taylor: pages 50, 71, 72.

PUBLISHED SOURCES

Drummond, John D, *A River Runs to War*, W.H. Allen Ltd. London, 1960.
Heavey, William F., *Down Ramp! The Story of the Army Amphibian Engineers*, Infantry Journal Press, Washington, 1947.
Howarth, D., *The Shetland Bus*, Shetland Times Ltd., Lerwick, 1998.
Howe, George F., *Northwest Africa: Seizing the Initiative in the West*, Government Printing Office, Washington DC, 1957.
Longmate, N. *The GIs*, Hutchinson, London.
Roscoe, Theodore, *US Submarine Operations in World war II*, US Naval Institute.
Royal Engineers Journal, March 1958.
Seymour, William, *British Special Forces*, Sidgewick & Jackson Ltd., London 1985
Shaffner, T.P, LL.D., *History of the United States of America*, London Printing and Publishing Co., London and New York.
USN Civil Engineer Corps, *Building the Navy's Bases in World War II*, US Government Printing Office, Washington, DC
Van Der Vat, D., *The Atlantic Campaign*, Hodder & Stoughton, London, 1988.

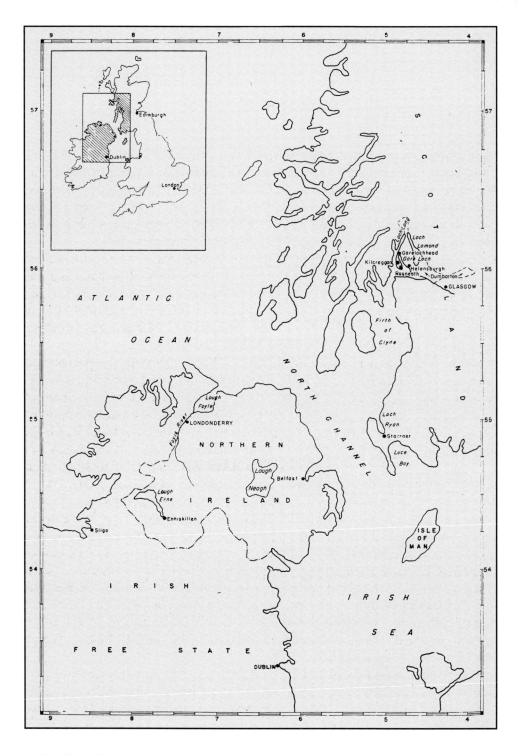

Irish and Scottish Bases.

PREFACE

Situated on a small peninsula formed by the Clyde Estuary, the Gareloch and Loch Long, Rosneath had an important part to play in Word War II, yet the wartime events at Rosneath are now all but forgotten. There are few references and little material available locally on the construction and operation of US Navy Base Two at Rosneath and its important contribution to US Navy operations in the Eastern Atlantic and the successful amphibious landings in North-West Africa, Italy and France.

With the assistance of official records made available by various United States archival departments, I have attempted to set down the course of events at Rosneath Base during the years 1941–45, which I hope will reveal the importance of wartime events on Garelochside, pay tribute to the civilian American engineers and Royal Engineers who built Base II, the US and other forces who served or trained here and the generosity of local people who extended a warm welcome and support to all the Allied forces who were their guests.

I am indebted to the archivists and historians in the United States who replied promptly and generously to my constant enquiries, and in particular I must thank the following: Vernon R. Smith, Stuart L. Butler, Kenneth D. Slessinger, Gibson Bell Smith and the staff of the National Archives, Washington DC. Also Vincent A. Transano PhD and Carol Marsh of the Naval Construction Center, Port Hueneme California, Bernard F. Cavalcante and David Manning of the Washington Navy Yard Historical Branch and Lieutenant-Commander T. Henn of the Groton Submarine Base, Groton, Connecticut. My thanks are also due to the staff of the following for their help: Public Records Office, London, the Imperial War Museum, London, the Mitchell Library, Glasgow, Dumbarton Library, Helensburgh Library and Rosneath Library.

In addition, I have spoken to the local people and others who remember Rosneath and district in wartime and must express my gratitude to all of them and in particular to those who kindly provided personal photographs and other momentoes of these years. My thanks also go to the following who generously provided accounts of their war service experience at Rosneath: Tom Fulton (ex-RE) who provided invaluable details of the early construction period at Rosneath, Ted Humes (ex-USN) who supplied recollections of his service at Base Two and the following US veterans who kindly provided their memories of wartime days at Rosneath: R. Drake, D.J. Gavine, R.C. Key, S.P. Maresca, R.J. Motherwell, R.J. Morrissey, J.C. Parker, E. Strobel, H.A. Singleton, J. Tsepas, and W.K. Walters.

Acknowledgement is also due to the following for their kind permission to refer to or quote from copyright material: the estate of David Howarth for *The Shetland Bus* by David Howarth; Curtis Brown Ltd, London, for *The Atlantic Campaign* by Dan van der Vat; the US Naval Institute for *US Submarines in World War II* by Theodore Roscoe; Hutchinson, London, for *The GIs* by Norman Longmate; the Government Printing Office, Washington, for *Northwest Africa: Seizing the Initiative in the West* by George F. Howe.

ABBREVIATIONS

AA	Anti Aircraft	RA	Royal Artillery
ARC	American Red Cross	RAF	Royal Air Force
ATS	Auxiliary Territorial Service	RCN	Royal Canadian Navy
BMC	Boat Maintenance Company	RCT	Regimental Combat Team
C in C	Commander in Chief	RE	Royal Engineers
COP	Combined Operations Pilotage	RN	Royal Navy
ENSA	Entertainments National Services Association	SBS	Special Boat Service
		TA	Territorial Army
ETO	European Theatre of Operations	TAF	Temporary Air Facilities
GI	Government Issue (US soldier)	UK	United Kingdom
HMS	His Majesty's Ship	US	United States
LCA	Landing Craft Assault	USAAF	United States Army Air Force
LCF	Landing Craft Flak	USN	United States Navy
LCG	Landing Craft Gun	USNAF	United States Navy Amphibious Force
LCM	Landing Craft Mechanised		
LCT	Landing Craft Tank	USNCB	United States Navy Construction Battalion
LCVP	Landing Craft Vehicle and Personnel		
		USO	United Services Organisation
LST	Landing Ship Tank	USS	United States Ship
Lt	Lieutenant	WAAF	Women's Auxiliary Air Force
Lt Cmdr	Lieutenant Commander	WRNS	Women's Royal Naval Service
NI	Northern Ireland	WVS	Women's Voluntary Service
O in C	Officer in Charge	YMCA	Young Men's Christian Association

ONCE MORE TO WAR

When Her Royal Highness, Princess Louise, Duchess of Argyll, died on 3 December 1939, Britain was for the second time in the 20th century at war with Germany. The death of the Princess ended Rosneath's royal connection and in early 1940, some four and a half centuries of Argyll family ownership also came to an end when Rosneath Estate was sold.

As in the 1914 war, troops arrived in the district but military priorities had changed. The German occupation of western Europe brought new dangers of aerial attack to the industries and urban populations of Clydeside, no longer protected by distance from enemy airfields and the limited range of early bombers. Anti-aircraft units were accordingly among the first military forces to arrive on the peninsula.

The 421st Battery, 57th Searchlight Regiment, Royal Artillery, Territorial Army (TA), set up their generator and searchlight above Cove in December 1940. They depended on a hillside stream for water but enjoyed the luxury of meals prepared by girls of the Women's Auxiliary Territorial Service (ATS) quartered in Inverclyde House. Other anti-aircraft positions were established at Camsail, Rosneath and on the Peaton hillside overlooking the Gareloch.

The 421st Battery.

Construction of Faslane Military Port begins.

Wharf construction underway – Faslane.

South end Faslane wharf.

One Rosneath resident remembers the Camsail battery in action and his family's apprehension whenever the air-raid alert siren sounded since they feared the collapse of their house ceilings from the blast of the nearby gun almost as much as the thought of falling bombs. Fortunately, the peninsula batteries were not often in action since Clydeside did not experience the expected frequency of air attacks despite the heavy raids on Clydebank and Greenock in 1941 due to the Luftwaffe's main strength being committed to the invasion of Russia.

Rosneath peninsula had escaped lightly during these raids. Several parachute mines exploded in a field near Portkil, and local children later collected shrapnel and pieces of parachute as souvenirs. Some can recall being allowed to watch air-raids in progress from the comparative safety of house doorways. The spectacle of tracer bullets, probing searchlight beams, exploding shells and the distant flash of exploding bombs was an unforgettable experience. They were, however, reminded of the dangerous reality as a constant stream of falling shrapnel from anti-aircraft (AA) shell bursts ripped through nearby trees and the thunder of bomb and gun-fire echoed around the hills.

In addition to army personnel, naval crews had arrived to man yachts that had been requisitioned by the Admiralty. McKellar's yard at Kilcreggan, J.A. Silver's at Rosneath and McGruer's at Clynder prepared these vessels for patrol duties and throughout the war years would build many craft for the Royal Navy.

Home Guard units were formed – the Rosneath platoon under the command of Acting Lieutenant James McGruer of Clynder. Air-raid wardens were appointed, fire-fighting and mine-watching groups organised and observation posts set up for night-time manning. Home Guardsmen were paid a token sum for overnight duties, and the local platoon elected to pool their earnings in a refreshment fund for occasional convivial evenings at their Achnashie Coach-house headquarters to which locally based service personnel were cordially invited.

Despite the war, most peninsula folk went about their normal tasks as usual, but for the village youth, especially the girls, rural life became more exciting as young soldiers and sailors appeared in their midst and local dances held increasing promise. The presence of ATS girls likewise provided local males with a determined desire to learn the latest dance steps. Accustomed to the usual village 'hop' where country dancing had prevailed, and shy of asking local girls to attempt modern dances, the young village males were delighted to find that the army girls were perfectly willing to partner them and demonstrate up-to-date ballroom skills.

Clachan House, former dower house of the Argyll family, became a temporary barracks for the Royal Engineers who arrived in late 1940 to build a new military port in Faslane Bay. The rambling, draughty old building provided shelter for the troops until accommodation was prepared at Stuckenduff and on site at Faslane. The new arrivals were given solemn warnings by villagers to beware of the Grey Lady of Clachan House who reputedly haunted the old house on moonlit nights before making her ghostly way along Yew Tree Avenue to the crypt in the nearby ancient village graveyard. On one such night, a young soldier awoke to an eerie and intermittent rattling sound in the corridor, which slowly increased in volume as it neared the door of the room in which by now almost every man was apprehensively wide-awake. Arming themselves with whatever came to hand, several brave souls, acting as one, threw the door open to be confronted by the cook-house cat clutching a large marble between its paws.

The construction of the Military Port at Faslane had been proposed in 1940 following the British Expeditionary Force's withdrawal from France. Southern English ports were virtually closed to shipping because of enemy air and naval activity, and while the Rivers Clyde and Mersey became the nation's major import terminals, Faslane Bay was selected as the site for the new military port. Some five thousand Royal Engineers and Pioneer Corps personnel worked around the clock, seven days a week, during the construction period, ably assisted by ATS girls who served as cooks, clerical staff and drivers. Faslane Military Port No.1 was officially opened on 8 August 1942 by the Secretary of State for War Transport.

Another new development on the Gareloch was the relocation of the Aircraft Experimental Establishment (AEE) from Felixstowe in Suffolk, now vulnerable to enemy attack, to the relative safety of Rhu Bay. Flying-boat hangars were built on the foreshore near Rhu Pier and houses requisitioned for Royal Air Force personnel and civilian staff. The new establishment worked on many different problems: designing and testing air-launched missiles; improving anti-submarine depth charges; testing new aircraft and evaluating new survival equipment for 'downed' aircrews. A further development from the AEE's work at Rhu was the construction of the Hydro-Ballistic Research Station in Glen Fruin and the later missile-testing unit at Coulport.

Meanwhile, at Rosneath, the pace of rural life continued more or less as normal until, in the summer of 1941, the village was rudely aroused from its torpor by the arrival of a new group of Royal Engineers (REs), closely followed by civilian contractors from the United States, who immediately began work on a carefully planned construction programme.

Launch of HDML 1089 at McGruer's Yard, Clynder, 1940.

CHAPTER 1

BRITISH/AMERICAN CO-OPERATION AT ROSNEATH

In 1941, Betty McGruer of Clynder joined the Women's Royal Naval Service (WRNS) for duty with the degaussing station at Portkil, near Kilcreggan. Five 'Wrens', including Betty, were quartered in nearby accommodation and two civilians operated the station electrical equipment. The girls gathered the data and forwarded it to headquarters staff at HMS *Revlis*, Ardencaple Castle, Helensburgh.

Wren McGruer invariably cycled home to Clynder when off duty, taking a shortcut across the policies of Rosneath Estate and around the empty Rosneath House. One summer day in 1941, pedalling through the estate gardens, she suddenly and quite unexpectedly found herself in the midst of a village of army tents with soldiers everywhere. The troops were equally surprised at the sudden appearance of a lone Wren cycling through their camp, but, quickly recovering, they shouted approval and whistled encouragingly as Betty peddled on, convinced that she had encountered the entire British Army. Wren McGruer, in fact, had just met the 996 Dock Operating Company, Royal Engineers, newly arrived from the south of England.

During that same summer of 1941, Mrs McKay of Rosneath had been enjoying a pleasant evening walk with friends in the vicinity of Clachan House when they happened upon a group of civilian men speaking together in American accents. The villagers wondered why visitors from the neutral United States were in Rosneath but knew nothing of recent, highly secret discussions in distant Washington, DC, and of the momentous decisions reached there that had brought the Americans to the village and would soon bring unprecedented activity and change to Garelochside.

From the outbreak of war in 1939, Britain and France had sought military aid from the United States. President Franklin D. Roosevelt was sympathetic to Britain's plight and eager to help, but the 1934 Johnson Act and the Neutrality Acts of 1939 prohibited American financial or material aid being given to warring foreign nations. The President persuaded the US Congress to modify the laws, however, thereby allowing Britain to buy vital supplies on a cash-only basis. The President's policy was a matter of profound relief to the British Government, but the Treasury could not afford to continue purchasing American arms, food and fuel in the amounts necessary for survival. In 1940, Britain's leaders had recognised that without 'massive and growing American support' continued resistance to the German threat did not seem possible and it appeared that the British people would be starved into submission if further extensive American aid was not obtained.

Prime Minister Winston Churchill had asked President Roosevelt, as a matter of urgency, for fifty obsolete United States Navy (USN) destroyers to aid the Royal Navy (RN) and Royal Canadian Navy (RCN) in their fight against enemy submarines, warning that it might not be possible to pay for them before delivery. In June, legal experts advised the American Government that it could 'dispose of surplus weaponry as it saw fit', and the way now seemed open for an ever increasing flow of supplies and arms to beleaguered Britain. In August the President's advisers warned that he could not give away such equipment to a foreign power but that it could be legally bartered. The President consequently offered to exchange the destroyers for the lease of naval base sites in Newfoundland and in the Caribbean.

By the end of 1940, Britain's financial reserves were almost exhausted and her future remained bleak. On 9 March 1941, however, the Lend-Lease Bill was passed by Congress allowing the President to 'exchange, lease or lend materials to any foreign country which he deemed was essential to the security of the United States'. The problem of imminent British financial collapse was averted, but the threat from German naval and air forces continued and invasion remained a dangerous possibility. American assistance, despite the USA's continuing neutrality, now included USN escorts to mid-Atlantic for UK-bound convoys and increasingly Americans admired Britain's continued defiance of Nazi Germany.

The President's actions made eventual American involvement in the conflict appear ever more likely, and in early 1941, at a series of meetings in Washington, it was agreed that 'advance' US bases, financed by the Lend-Lease agreement, would be built in Britain by American engineers. An initial $50,000,000 was allocated by Congress, and in March 1941 Captain L. Denfeld, USN, was dispatched to Britain, as a civilian, to seek suitable sites for the proposed bases. Four were selected: Londonderry in Northern Ireland and Rosneath in Scotland as naval bases; Lough Erne in Northern Ireland and Loch Ryan in Scotland as naval air-squadron stations.

In keeping with its neutral status, the US Government engaged American civilian construction personnel to build the new bases in Britain. Two construction companies, George A. Fuller Inc. and Merritt Chapman & Scott Inc., were combined under the general designation Temporary Aviation Facilities (TAF) and secretly transported to the United Kingdom in British ships during the summer of 1941. A week before the contracts were signed on 12 June 1941, the officer in charge of the USN Civil Engineer Corps, in civilian dress, arrived in Northern Ireland to prepare for the imminent arrival of the contractors and their equipment. Around 1,150 American construction engineers duly arrived in Northern Ireland and Scotland in the summer of 1941, along with many shiploads of materials, heavy machinery and vehicles. Quickly settling in, they began working with 'a concentration of effort not familiar to this country'. A labour force amounting to nearly five thousand men was recruited in Ireland and distributed among the various sites, with additional workers being recruited locally as necessary.

Greenock and Liverpool were now the main UK terminals for vital imports, and Londonderry was invaluable as a 'turn-around' base for convoy escort ships because of its situation near the North Western Approaches. Consequently, the Americans gave initial priority to the Londonderry project: the building of Base One for the repair and servicing of destroyers and other escort vessels. Rosneath, the other major naval base site selected by Captain Denfeld, was designated Base Two and would be similar to Base One with the addition of facilities for submarines.

18

On 12 July 1941, five USN Civil Engineer Corps officers, in civilian dress, arrived at Rosneath to find a detachment of Royal Engineers busily engaged in building a new pier north of Clynder. On the 27th, a coaster arrived from Londonderry laden with construction equipment, part of the initial shipment of TAF material from the United States. The REs unloaded this cargo at their new jetty in readiness for the arrival of eleven Americans on 7 August. On the 10th, a further 150 TAF technicians arrived, followed on the 13th by a similar number of Irish labourers.

Shortly before the appearance of the first Americans at Rosneath, as Wren McGruer had discovered, the 996 Dock Operating Company, RE, had arrived to set up their tented camp in the gardens around Rosneath House. The 996 Company had escaped from Brest as the Germans overran France in 1940, and after a spell in the south of England recovering and regrouping they were dispatched to Rosneath under the command of Major J.W. Richardson, an expert in ships and shipping from years of prewar experience with the British India Steam Navigation Company.

The REs were curious as to the logic of being posted to what seemed to them such a remote area, since the unit was a highly skilled team of dock-operating and stevedoring experts many of whom had worked in the London docks before the war. There seemed little obvious need for their talents in Rosneath, and they were surprised when joined by the American civilians who took up residence at Rosneath House and spent their days surveying the lands and shores of Rosneath Estate. When villagers questioned the soldiers they received the evasive answer that it was 'just an

TAF road builders in forest, Rosneath, 1941.

19

TAF materials near Rosneath House, 1941. Royal Engineer tents in the background.

exercise', but the REs were able to use their skills fully when, on 17 August, the first of many shiploads of construction plant arrived directly from the United States and was unloaded at the newly built RE pier. Vast amounts of equipment, materials and supplies were received: trucks, bulldozers, generators, diesel cranes, 60-foot logs for pier building, parts for storage sheds and Quonset huts (the insulated and well-heated American version of the British Nissen) indeed everything necessary for the rapid construction of a modern military township including food supplies for the work-force. On occasions when particularly heavy items arrived they were transferred into barges at Greenock by dockside cranes and towed across the Clyde to Rosneath.

In charge of the Americans was Harry Bowles, a very energetic and courteous gentleman who always seemed to know when cargo ships from Quonset Point Naval Base in the USA would arrive. He was assisted by four senior civil engineers and by the skilled tradesmen of the TAF who were quartered at Rosneath House and in various rented properties around the peninsula. The Americans soon became quite well known to, and largely accepted by, the local people. A few villagers still remember individuals such as Bill Pasano, Arthur Gallagher, Frank Grady, Dave Stiles, Phil Arundel, Si Lamarr and others. The RE officers were awarded honorary membership of the TAF commissariat in Rosneath House where they enjoyed the privilege of buying American chocolate, cigarettes and other such luxuries that were severely rationed in wartime Britain.

The REs organised concerts, football games and boxing matches involving TAF men and fellow REs from the Faslane Port construction site. Local residents were overwhelmed with dancing opportunities as never before. On 24 July 1941, the 996 Company organised a dance in Rosneath Hall, which, according to a report in the *Helensburgh and Gareloch Times*, was 'filled to capacity'. On the same night local Royal Artillery (RA) units held a special late dance at the Burgh Hall in Cove, which was 'enjoyed by capacity patrons dancing to the RA orchestra of seven pieces playing up-to-date music'. On 20 August, the local newspaper reported that during the week, dances had taken place on Tuesday, Thursday and Friday in Rosneath Village Hall, the Thursday event being a 'carnival evening'. On the Saturday, an open-air dance was held by the REs on the lawn at Rosneath House with a special motor-ferry service across the Gareloch provided for the convenience of Helensburgh patrons.

In early September 1941, the fife and drum band of the 996 Dock Operating Company, RE, from Rosneath, by kind permission of Major Richardson, contributed to the local events of the annual 'Dunbartonshire Week'. They marched from the cross-roads at Rosneath village to Clynder Hotel and enlivened the afternoon with musical selections as villagers and servicemen enjoyed a regatta, ably organised from the hotel jetty by local man William McGruer. It was a day of warm sunshine with a light breeze, and the starting line in front of the hotel was 'gay with white, red and tan sails'. A launch was available for boat trips on the loch, and the success of this innovation was evident in the constant queue of prospective customers.

Military units stationed around the lochside and in Helensburgh also organised many dances: the Royal Navy at Cairndhu and at Cove; No.6 Commando in Helensburgh; the Royal Engineers and Pioneer Corps at Faslane; and the Royal Air Force at Rhu. Weekly 'Services' events in Helensburgh's Victoria Hall, organised by Mrs Blythe with assistance from a group of local ladies, were also well attended, with the popular Bill Brehenny Band supplying the music, often aided by individual musicians from various military units stationed in the area. The highlight of each event was the interval, when the ladies served tea and sandwiches, always well received by the service personnel present.

The *Helensburgh and Gareloch Times* of 10 September 1941 reported that 'there was a large attendance at the swimming pond for the Services Swimming Gala' with competing teams from locally stationed navy, airforce and army units, including girls from the three women's services. An added attraction was 'a short but thrilling display by the RAF with a number of Sunderland flying-boats which roared powerfully both high and low in the air'.

TAF engineer with Indian motor cycle, Rosneath, 1941.

TAF-built air-raid shelter, Rosneath, 1941.

Despite such pleasant social distractions, the serious business of military training and emergency war construction work continued around Garelochside. At Rosneath, formerly quiet rural roads had become busy with a variety of American vehicles: Mack, Dodge and Chevrolet trucks, pickups and cars; station wagons, Indian motorcycles with sidecars, even American bicycles. Bulldozers, graders, dumpers and various other items of modern American construction equipment now roared around the former estate fields and woodlands where 'pick and shovel' methods had previously prevailed. In the midst of severe British rationing, the Americans had petrol aplenty, and business visitors to the TAF headquarters, parking their cars alongside American vehicles, were pleasantly surprised to find their car tanks 'topped up' by the gasolene truck, which appeared to drive around all day filling up everything in sight.

The Americans at first had been inclined to belittle the British war effort and teased the REs with comments like 'you were caught with your pants down at Dunkirk' and how, if given the chance, 'they would soon sort things out'. They were careless about the blackout and not very security-minded, but following the Japanese attack of 7 December 1941 on the USN Base at Pearl Harbor and the consequent American involvement in the war, a remarkable transformation took place at Rosneath. On 8 December, Harry Bowles and his senior management team arrived at their desks in Rosneath House resplendent in naval uniform. He was, in fact, Lieutenant-Commander Bowles of the USN Civil Engineer Corps and his four senior assistants blossomed forth as lieutenants, their desks now adorned with fancy bronze nameplates revealing their naval rank. The newly emerged USN officers now became very concerned regarding security matters, and the REs were asked to provide extra guards and sentries all over the place since the Americans had no 'other ranks' to perform such duties at that time.

Despite the secrecy surrounding the American activities at Rosneath, by September 1941 the *Helensburgh and Gareloch Times* was reporting the frequent instances of labourers, drivers, welders, mechanics or soldiers 'from Rosneath' forfeiting bail money in the local law court in Helensburgh for a variety of minor offences: being drunk and incapable, committing a nuisance, breach of the peace, or parking violations. One report confirmed that Williams Jenning Beattie, master mechanic from Rosneath, was fined ten shillings plus five shillings expenses for 'leaving his vehicle without lights in Colquhoun Square on 4 November 1941'.

The period was one of continuous rainfall, and the *Times* further reported that the 'guests' at Rosneath 'have had a new coat of arms designed. The emblem is a duck with an umbrella and gumboots'. Another article informed readers in September 1941 that Robert Montgomery, the well-known Hollywood film actor, 'is on duty in the district and expected at a local dance one of these evenings'. On 11 March 1942, a further article mentioned that:

> under the auspices of the Americans stationed in the district, a very successful and
> enjoyable dance was held in the Burgh Hall, Cove, on Monday when there was a
> large attendance of patrons which taxed the hall to capacity. An appetising purvey
> was carried out by the organisers and the dance music was all that could be desired.

Estate farmland surrounding the village of Rosneath had been requisitioned by the Government for the new base, and the fields of the recently ejected tenants, the Calderwood family, were

Lt Tom Fulton, 996 Dock Operating Company, Royal Engineers, Rosneath, August-December 1941.

soon churned to mud by the heavy American machinery. One field of turnips was rapidly 'harvested' as the TAF men bulldozed the crop into a muddy heap in a corner of the field. Road-building material was urgently required to overcome the mud problem, but the nearest quarry was some twenty-five miles distant, over the narrow, tortuous lochside roads. Sophisticated rock-crushing equipment was obtained as a priority, and a quarry was opened at Camsail, adjacent to the site of Base Two's new industrial area. Road building now proceeded rapidly, and many miles of high-quality tarmacadam were quickly laid and modern drainage installed. Work areas were concreted to eliminate the mud hazard.

Lt Fulton, RE remembers well the night when a ferocious storm swept the Gareloch. Ships moored in the loch were blown ashore, and a corral near Clynder Pier, holding thousands of piles shipped from the USA for the Rosneath wharves, was breached, allowing piles to drift around and out of the Gareloch. During the next week or so, TAF men and REs in motor launches spent their days rounding up maverick piles from around the Firth of Clyde and towing them to Rosneath Bay where pile-drivers waited to begin the building of a new and extensive wharf system.

The lieutenant recalls another event at Rosneath when a merchant ship laden with TAF materials had anchored in the bay to await unloading by army stevedores. When the soldiers were detailed to their various cargo-unloading tasks, it was customary for the RE officers in charge to gather on the open upper bridge of the vessel where they would join the ship's officer of the watch for a 'wee refreshment' while keeping an eye on deck activities below. On this occasion, the young third mate on duty was asked the purpose of several robust-looking metal boxes that were mounted on the upper bridge. Explaining that they contained the ship's anti-aircraft defence system, which fired coils of wire into the air to entrap low-flying enemy planes, he added that they had not as yet needed to be used but that the procedure was really quite simple. Walking across the bridge to a nearby lever, he pulled it to demonstrate.

To the surprise of all, the lids flew off the steel boxes with an ear-splitting roar, and amidst flame and dense clouds of black smoke, coils of seemingly endless steel wire shot skywards high above the ship before falling in heaps around the bridge and decks, draping the masts and rigging and breaking the ship's radio aerials. Luckily nobody was injured apart from temporary shock and deafness among members of the bridge party and those working on deck below.

Everyone had been severely shaken, especially the 'third'. He had mistakenly assumed that the explosive charges had been removed from the apparatus when the ship entered port. It took some considerable time to retrieve and restow the wire, repair the aerials and generally tidy ship. Fortunately, the master's comments on his junior officer were not logged.

In addition to their normal duties, the soldiers sometimes became involved in various non-military operations. On one such day, when fire broke out in the TAF kitchen at Rosneath House, the soldiers went into action with their emergency fire fighting equipment. Pumps were rushed into position and hoses led to the nearby loch for water but despite energetic cranking of starting handles, the pump engines refused to start. Meantime, the Americans had dealt with the blaze using portable extinguishers and when the excitement was over it was discovered that the fire-pump fuel tanks had been empty.

On another occasion, when the TAF's Irish labour force went on strike for higher pay, the REs were called on to help control the situation. Armed with pick handles, the soldiers were hidden amongst nearby trees and bushes while pay negotiations took place between the American labour manager, Mr Norfleet, and the striking workers. Fortunately, an amicable settlement was agreed and the troops were able to withdraw quietly.

Relations between Americans and Irish were sometimes strained and the REs would have to act as referees. The TAF used open work-boats to provide a ferry service for their men between Helensburgh Pier and Castle Point, Rosneath. On one particular late-night passage from Helensburgh, the boat was well laden, with Irish forward, Americans and Royal Engineers aft. A particularly well-built American, with perhaps a drink or two too many in him, took exception to a remark from one of the Irish and made his way forward to remonstrate. A group of RE officers felt duty-bound to intervene, since an open boat at night in mid-channel was not the safest place for a general melee. Acting as one, the military men downed the protesting American and sat on him for the remainder of the voyage.

By the end of 1941, the initial construction phase at Rosneath was well under way, and the RE Dock Operating Company, no longer needed at Rosneath, was transferred to the Combined Operations Base at Inveraray. Commander Bowles was relieved as Officer in Charge, Rosneath, on 27 January 1942 for important duties elsewhere and was replaced by his assistant, Lt M.R. Montgomery. On 7 March, the first ship to use the new Rosneath wharf came alongside to discharge cargo as Base Two neared readiness for war duties.

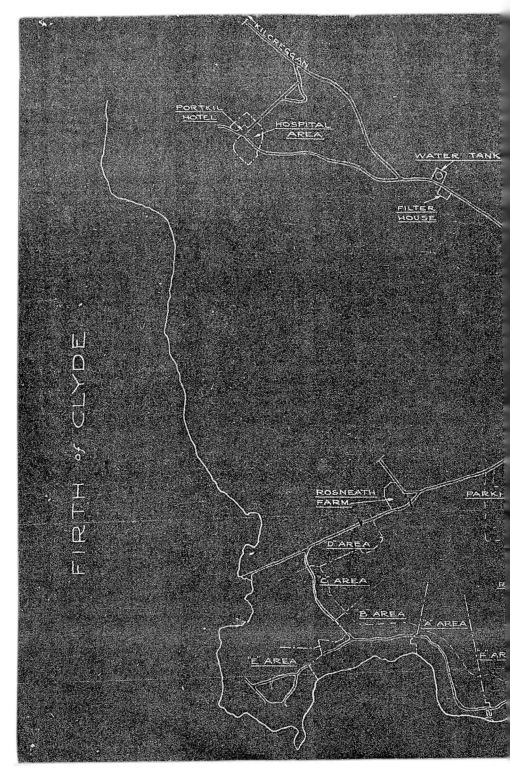

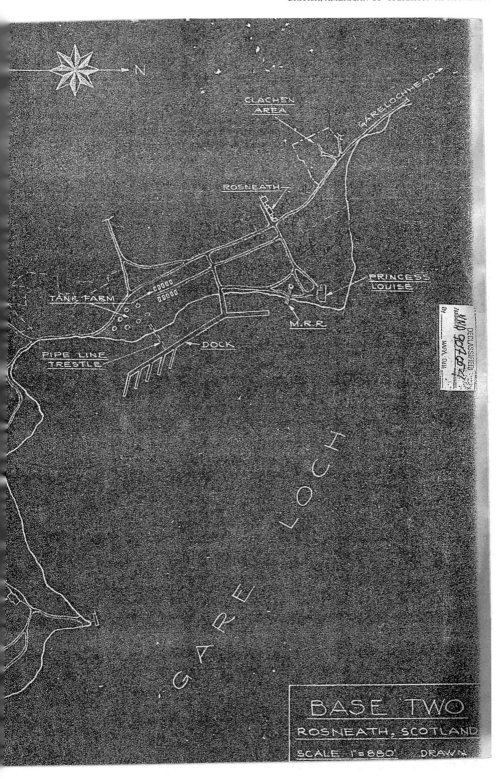

Construction phase at Rosneath Base Industrial Area 1941-42.

USN station wagon entering north gate, Rosneath Base, at Ferry Road. Village and school in the background.

CHAPTER 2

READY FOR ACTION AT ROSNEATH

Following the entry of the United States into the war in December 1941, the original plans for Rosneath had been altered and the proposed facilities were cut by about one third. The proposal to extend Base Two northwards beyond the village of Clynder to provide extra docking and maintenance for destroyers was cancelled and other planned support services at Rosneath – such as the hospital and the tank farm for oil storage – reduced in size. During April and May 1942, as construction work reached its peak, 325 Americans, a labour force of some 1,000 Irish and 250 locally recruited workers were employed at Rosneath. As the modified construction programme neared completion and since the USN had no immediate use at that time for the new facility, the Royal Navy occupied part of Base Two which was commissioned as HMS *Louisburg*, a Combined Operations establishment and convoy escort-ship repair depot.

US Naval Base, Rosneath, industrial and storage area.

US Naval Base, Rosneath, living huts.

Rosneath village was now an isolated civilian outpost surrounded by a self-sufficient naval township. Security control points with manned barriers were positioned on the main road at Mill Brae above Portkil and at Stroul Brae near Clynder. Residents of Rosneath village were given special passes, and no civilian without a pass was allowed off the local bus within the controlled area. The new docks system of 4,750 linear feet of deep-water pier and 1,500 linear feet of shallow berthing now formed the main port area. Four finger piers for submarines at the south end of the main pier and some sixty berths for assault landing craft were ready for use. A submarine degaussing pier was built in Stroul Bay, and a marine railway for amphibious landing craft maintenance was constructed near the old Rosneath Pier. A nearby RN-operated floating dock was available for larger vessels and submarines. The recently finished tank farm contained four fuel oil tanks, each of 100,000-barrel capacity, three diesel tanks holding 10,000 barrels apiece, ten 14,400-barrel-capacity gasolene tanks, and heating-oil storage. A pipeline system from the tank farm to the main wharf allowed for the refuelling of vessels lying alongside.

The American engineers renovated and enlarged the long-disused estate mill-water system at Mill Brae on the Kilcreggan road to provide a supply of some ten million gallons. The local people had always depended on hillside streams and wells for their water, but the Americans declared such sources unfit for human use and installed a filtration and sterilization plant for the Base supply. The original and now derelict TAF filter shed still stands to the left at Mill Brae on the road from Rosneath to Kilcreggan. A village resident remarked at the time that:

> we had never thought there was anything wrong with our water. It was peat-stained during wet weather, but no one thought of it as a health hazard. On the contrary, we liked it, indeed preferred it to all other tap water, except that of Glasgow. When we discovered that the Americans drank about fifteen large cups of coffee daily we wondered if perhaps such over indulgence was not an equal, even greater hazard to health than our water.

Personnel accommodation had initially been built around Clachan House, and several large refrigerated storage sheds, with their own generating plants, were situated in Clachan Park between Clachan House and Rosneath village. These storage sheds were soon filled with frozen meat and other items of food which by 1942 were but a memory to most local residents. The main Base accommodation area was well concealed in the heavily wooded Green Isle area to the south of Rosneath House and was divided into sections A, B, C, D, E and F. Each section contained groups of fifty Quonset huts, each accommodating ten men, with a 'galley' at the centre of every group. Underground air-raid shelters were distributed around the entire area along with miscellaneous service huts, including several for religious use.

Portkil, near Kilcreggan, was the site of a two-hundred-bed naval hospital, consisting of sixty-eight Quonset huts specially adapted for medical use and arranged in a fan-shape around the central galley units. The huts were connected by paved, covered walkways, allowing patients to be moved even in the wettest of weather. The main walkway was promptly signposted 'Broadway' when US Naval medical personnel arrived in 1942. Nearby Portkil House and Cottage provided living quarters for the medical officers.

US Navy Hospital, Portkil, 1942-45.

USN Medical Officers, Portkil Hospital.

US Naval Base, Rosneath. Living huts for hospital personnel, August 1944.

Portkil Hospital Medical Hut with naval staff.

USN Magazine Area construction, Peaton, overlooking Loch Long, 1942.

Portkil House. USN Medical Officer accommodation, Portkil Hospital.

Ammunition magazines were situated underground on the west-facing slope of Peaton Hill near Coulport, well away from residential areas. Fourteen 50 x 20-foot steel-lined bunkers were set into the hillside to hold ammunition and explosives. Throughout the main Base areas a total of 749 Quonset huts, 8 utility buildings, 17 storage sheds, 153 air-raid shelters and 25 steel magazines were erected, including those at Peaton Hill. Several private houses around the peninsula that had been requisitioned for TAF staff accommodation were retained for naval officers when the civilian contract ended. Ferry Road and the Ferry Inn at Rosneath had remained open to civilians during the construction phase but were closed to public access in early 1942 and incorporated within the Base perimeter. In June 1942, when the USN officially occupied Rosneath Base, the Ferry Inn and annexe became the officers' club and was renamed 'Princess Louise' in tribute to the late Royal Princess.

A Rosneath resident recalled his first invitation to the Princess Louise for drinks and his amazement when he and his wife discovered that, on requesting a gin and tonic, the duty bartender brought them a full bottle of gin, tonic water, ice cubes and glasses. Orders from others around the table were dealt with in a similar fashion and each group refilled their glasses as necessary from their bottle, a source of wonder to local people unfamiliar with American ways and conditioned by carefully measured British drinking habits and wartime shortages.

The Ferry Inn had served as a military hospital during the 1914-18 war but was not needed

Free French leader General Charles de Gaulle visits French wounded at Knockderry Hospital, Cove 1942.

as such during the second war. Knockderry Castle, Cove, however was requisitioned as an emergency centre for service patients. In 1942, it was occupied by wounded Free French naval personnel who were greatly honoured on Christmas Eve when General De Gaulle, leader of the Free French Forces in Britain, arrived to distribute gifts and spend an hour or so with the patients. Subsequent newspaper reports revealed that the Secretary of State for Scotland would have attended personally to welcome the French leader but for the short notice of the visit. The Scottish Health Department Secretary however arrived to welcome the high-ranking visitor. Local man Tom McNeilage clearly remembers the day when he drove one of his father's taxis which had been hired to meet the General and his aides at Kilcreggan Pier and take them to Knockderry.

In addition to the loss of their local hotel, the residents of Rosneath had already lost their much loved passenger steamer, *Lucy Ashton*. She had served them well since 1909 as the regular Gareloch paddle-steamer. Berthed overnight at Garelochhead, *Lucy* would depart early each morning on the first of several daily voyages between Garelochhead and Craigendoran via the lochside piers. In September 1939, however, as a wartime economy measure, Garelochhead Pier was closed and the service to Craigendoran suspended. *Lucy Ashton* then became the sole Clyde passenger vessel remaining in civilian service, operating within the confines of the defensive Clyde anti-submarine boom until 1945, calling at Dunoon, Gourock, Craigendoran and Kilcreggan, steaming some 143,297 miles and carrying 1,128,258 passengers. On 18 March 1942, Rosneath Pier was closed to civilian traffic. The motor-ferry service to Rhu Point was transferred to Clynder Pier, from where it continued to operate across the Gareloch to a new pier at Gully Bridge. Waldie's local bus service from Helensburgh to Rhu village was extended to Gully Bridge for the convenience of ferry passengers.

PS Lucy Ashton *at Kilcreggan, 1942.*

As construction work at Rosneath neared completion, the British authorities, impressed by the TAF's abilities during their rapid construction of the Lend-Lease projects in Northern Ireland and Scotland, concluded that the highly efficient Americans could be advantageously employed on another essential project, the building of a new, deep-water oil station in the Clyde Estuary. As a result, after discussions with the American authorities, the wartime British Combined Petroleum Board and representatives of major US oil companies, the TAF contract was extended to include the construction of the proposed oil terminal and pipelines.

CHAPTER 3

FINNART OIL TERMINAL

In early 1942, a site for the new terminal was selected at Finnart further up Loch Long from Rosneath, with local assistance from the author's father, a retired shipmaster whose experience of the oil industry and knowledge of the Clyde Estuary's sea lochs was of considerable help. Plans were prepared, and the Americans started on the new contract in May 1942. Wasting no time, and using their sophisticated machinery to maximum effect, they cleared the route, dug trenches, welded together and buried sections of oil pipe at a rate that astonished local onlookers. Large trees standing in the way were pushed over and to one side by bulldozers without time-wasting sawing. In some sections the new pipeline had to be laid through private properties, and one local woman, in proud defiance of the imminent destruction of her beloved garden, stood firmly in the path of the bulldozer as it advanced towards her lawn. 'If I were you lady,' shouted the driver over the roar of his machine, 'I'd get the hell out of there cause this machine won't stop,' and it didn't. Two of the TAF workforce reached out and pulled the protesting woman to safety. A Clynder resident confidently awaited the advancing Americans as their bulldozers neared his property. He was convinced that if he spoke reasonably to the contractors they would tunnel carefully under his prized drystone wall, but his hopes were dashed when a machine struck from the adjoining garden and the wall disintegrated in a cloud of dust and flying stone. The Americans worked fast, and neither old stone walls nor gardeners would delay their progress. Nevertheless, on completing the pipe-laying operation, they repaired smashed walls and drains and replanted damaged hedges.

The new oil facility consisted of a deep-water pier and storage tanks connected by pipelines laid through Glen Fruin and the Vale of Leven to the oil terminal at Bowling. A short spur pipe-line extended the system to Old Kilpatrick, where it joined the existing Admiralty pipeline connection to the Grangemouth refinery. A seven mile long diesel fuel line connected Rosneath Base to Finnart. Temporary work camps were set up at Tullichewan Castle, Balloch and Bowling as work progressed.

The pipeline was designed for high-pressure operation and was the first such system to be installed in Britain eliminating the need for intermediate pumping stations. The twenty-five mile long line climbed from near sea level at both ends to over 600 feet where it crossed the hills at the head of Glen Fruin. Pumping capacity of 750 pounds per square inch was installed at Finnart and at Old Kilpatrick since the system was designed to flow in either direction. The American 'Detroit' diesel engines, original emergency power source for the pumping system installed in 1942, remain on site and in working order at Finnart. The tanker berth was built of reinforced concrete with a depth of thirty-five feet of water at low tide. Shore storage tanks of 110,000 barrels capacity, for fuel oil, with steam-heating facility, and 75,000 barrels of light-oil storage were installed. Because of the wet acid soils of the area, bitumastic felt protective coating was applied to all buried pipes, a special coating machine brought from the United States being used for this purpose.

The laying of the pipeline was difficult. Work began in August and constant rainfall was a problem. Lengths of pipe were welded together in the open air, despite the rain, and as each length was added, it was wrapped in the protective coating and lowered into the prepared trench by specially adapted bulldozers. The Americans, especially Texan oil experts among the TAF numbers, were not used to working in such persistent rainfall and built large welded steel umbrellas that were manhandled into position by labourers to provide shelter for the welders. Hard rock, drainage problems and the need in many sections to build access roads across peat bogs all added to the difficulties. Indeed, local rumour at the time insisted that a TAF bulldozer parked for the night on a peaty hillside had disappeared before daylight, presumably swallowed by the bog land.

As well as the Texan oil men, the TAF numbers included a few American Indians. On 4 July 1942, the Westerners celebrated American Independence Day by staging a traditional rodeo in a field near Rosneath House. The Texans had already aroused much local interest by habitually wearing stetson hats and high-heeled boots. They now treated the local villagers to their first Wild West Show. A number of horses were hired from Mae McHarg and Mae McCrorie of the Glasgow Street Riding School in Helensburgh. With the Indians and Westerners in traditional gear, the rodeo was open to local people who were entertained by an authentic display of spectacular horsemanship, including cattle handling with the aid of some locally borrowed heifers. Lariat and other roping skills were also demonstrated, along with horseshoe-throwing contests.

Pier and oil tanks at Finnart camp, April 1943.

Food and drinks were on the house, and local guests were intrigued by their first taste of American canned lager and what may have been Scotland's first barbecue as steaks and hot-dogs were grilled by the American cooks. Wren McGruer of Clynder, who had been transferred from her degaussing station post to join several other RN girls as clerical assistants with the TAF, remembers 4 July 1942 as an entertaining and exciting day. Douglas Haig of Rosneath was a guest at the rodeo and remembers standing with a friend, who was enjoying a cigarette, when a Texan bull-whip expert shouted, 'Don't move, Mac. I'm gonna take the ash off your smoke,' and with an almighty crack of his whip, from what appeared to be an impossible distance, the lash tip neatly removed the cigarette ash from under the startled spectator's nose.

As 1942 ended, Rosneath experienced something of a pause after the constant activity of the preceding months. The hard-working civilians of the TAF had nearly completed the Finnart contract, and on 6 January 1943 the *Helensburgh and Gareloch Times* reported on the magnificent children's party held by the Americans on Christmas Day in the 'mansion house' at Rosneath. Over 300 lochside schoolchildren were collected and entertained by the Americans. The mess halls were 'gaily decorated', there were 'carnival hats for all' and white-coated waiters served 'liberal helpings of vanilla ice-cream, sponge cake made with white flour, and other rare treats'. Santa Claus arrived to distribute gifts from the large decorated tree in the entrance hall, and each child received a savings book containing five shillings' worth of saving stamps. In addition to these generous gestures, over a thousand 'candy bars' were handed out, and the party ended with cheers and community singing led by one of the Americans.

By February 1943, the Finnart project awaited the arrival of special pumps and other equipment from the United States. The TAF's contract ended on 31 March and by 29 April, USN Construction Battalion personnel (Seabees) had taken over the final phase of the work. When the special equipment arrived in July 1943, the pipeline system was finished, tested and handed over to the British Combined Petroleum Board. One Seabee officer remained at Finnart until 31 July to instruct the British oilmen in the use and maintenance of the American equipment. The first echelon of thirteen officers and 725 men of the newly formed 29th Seabees had arrived at Rosneath on 30 November 1942. On 14 December 1942, the second echelon of fourteen officers and 282 men arrived to complete the Base Two Seabee maintenance force. Following completion of the Finnart contract, the Seabees took over remaining construction tasks at Rosneath.

In late 1942, shortly before the arrival of the Seabees, a group of TAF contractors had been temporarily transferred from Finnart to Rosneath Base where they maintained and renovated accommodation areas recently vacated by the Royal Navy in readiness for the imminent arrival of American military personnel. They also prepared new facilities: a fire-fighting school and practice beach landing areas at Rosneath and a small-arms firing range along the cliff face at Portkil near Kilcreggan. This was a direct result of high-level discussions between the British and American Chiefs of Staff in 1941 when the possibility of an Allied landing on the German-held coast of France was considered. It had been agreed that large numbers of American troops would be shipped to Britain – Operation Bolero – where they would train for an amphibious assault on the French coast. The Americans were of the opinion that by late summer 1942 a landing in strength – Operation Sledgehammer – could establish a foothold in France, followed by a full-scale invasion – Operation Roundup – in early 1943. These operations would require the construction of five USN amphibious training bases along the coast of southern England from Devon to Cornwall. Rosneath would act as the main receiving and assembly base for assault craft, crews and equipment as they arrived from the United States.

The first detachments of US troops had arrived in Northern Ireland in early 1942, and although eager to carry the fight directly to the enemy by an early invasion of France, the Americans were persuaded by the more cautious British that a direct assault on the French coast at that time would be costly and highly dangerous. Consequently, Sledgehammer and Roundup were cancelled and an alternative invasion of Vichy French North Africa, code-named Operation Torch, was proposed for late 1942.

MARITIME COMMAND
EUROPEAN THEATRE OF OPERATIONS
BASE TWO

August 27, 1942.

BASE ORDER NO. 1.

Subject: Establishment of Rosneath, Scotland, as a Naval Base
to be known as Base Two.

1.   Pursuant to instructions from the Commander-in-Chief, U.S.
Fleet, and by arrangement with the British Admiralty, the Naval Base at Rosneath,
Scotland, has been taken over by the U.S. Navy, as of Saturday, 22 August, 1942.
On 27 August, 1942, a formal turning over ceremony was held in which Rear Admiral
A. C. Bennett, U.S.N., officially received from Commodore Palmer, R.N., the Base
to be known as U.S. Navy Base Two. Detachments of British Navy, Army and Air
Force, and detachments of U.S. Navy and Army were present.

2.   Base Two was under the temporary command of Commander J. O.
Huse, U.S. Navy, until 27 August, 1942. On 27 August, 1942, Captain F. T.
Spellman, U.S. Navy, took temporary command of Base Two pending arrival of
regularly detailed Commanding Officer.

3.   This station will be administered in accordance with Naval
Regulations and customs; present station orders will remain in effect until
cancelled by my order.

F. T. SPELLMAN,
Captain, U.S. Navy,
Commanding Officer.

Copy to:
    SecNav.
    Cominch.
    Cinclant.
    Opnav.
    Comnaveau.

CHAPTER 4

ROSNEATH PREPARES FOR TORCH

In June 1942, the Joint Chiefs of Staff agreed that amphibious training for the large numbers of American troops then arriving in Britain was an urgent priority and that the bases at Londonderry and Rosneath would be ideal for this purpose. Accordingly, HMS *Louisburg* was decommisioned by the Royal Navy and taken over by the United States Navy with due ceremony on 22 August 1942 and commissioned as USN Base Two, Amphibious Training Establishment. Official reports of the hand-over refer to the 'very cordial relations' between American and British authorities during the transfer, noting that 'differences were smoothed out and co-operation attained, thus saving time and money for both governments'.

The amphibious assault practice beaches at Rosneath and the firefighting school set up by the TAF contractors were of great importance to the British-American training programme. Official dispatches, some originating from General Eisenhower, reveal the extent of beach assault training by US Army and Navy personnel at Rosneath in 1942. Following the American take-over at Rosneath, the Royal Navy continued to use the 'Internal Combustion Engine School' situated in the Base's industrial area. One hundred and fifty-six RN personnel attached to the school were fed and accommodated by the US Navy and given special access to Base facilities and leisure activities.

On 17 August, after an uneventful voyage from the United States, 7,500 enlisted men and 335 officers of the 1st US Army Engineer Amphibian Command's 1st Brigade arrived at Gourock where it was split among various locations in Scotland and Northern Ireland, with a battalion of the 591st Boat Regiment going to Rosneath. The commanding officer, Colonel Arnold, reported to London for a series of meetings while his second-in-command, Colonel Boatner, supervised the disembarkation and transfer of men and equipment to Base Two. The 1st Brigade was assigned to the Maritime Command of the USN Amphibious Forces, Atlantic Fleet Headquarters, under Admiral A.C. Bennet, USN, at Rosneath Base where the US Navy would operate the amphibious training centre. Colonel Wolfe would be responsible for assault training at Rosneath and at Londonderry, where a similar amphibious training centre had been established. Following visits to the Army units in Northern Ireland, Colonel Wolfe settled in at Rosneath on the Planning Staff of the now functioning Maritime Command.

The next few weeks were difficult for the Brigade since the Navy Maritime Command lacked experience of amphibious operations, trained personnel and equipment for amphibious training. The Brigade's proposal that qualified Army boat officers would teach landing craft operation to junior naval officers who would then train Brigade personnel was, perhaps understandably, not acceptable to the Navy. A shortage of landing craft because of an earlier high-level agreement giving the Royal Navy priority on new assault craft arriving from the United States also delayed progress. In addition, suitable rock-free practice landing beaches were rare at Rosneath and Inveraray. Toward Bay, near Loch Striven, had better beaches but no suitable barrack accommodation. The beach at Gailes in Ayrshire – selected as suitable for amphibious training by a party of RE officers from Inveraray, including Lt Fulton of the 996 was sandy and rock-free but exposure to the prevailing winds made it unusable in the frequently stormy weather. With few exceptions, the mainly rock-strewn shores around Inveraray and the Firth of Clyde necessitated a slow, careful approach by small assault craft to avoid damage from hidden rocks, rather than the rapid approach necessary if under enemy fire.

The British Combined Operations Training Centre at Inveraray, where US Army Regimental Combat Teams were undergoing joint amphibious training with British troops, was also being seriously curtailed by a shortage of serviceable assault craft because of a lack of maintenance personnel and spare parts. The 1st Brigade's Boat Maintenance Company (BMC) was consequently transferred temporarily from Rosneath to Inveraray, where its highly skilled engineers, armed with ample supplies of spare parts, carried out repairs 'to over a hundred British landing craft including a number returned in damaged condition from the Dieppe raid'. The BMC's expertise allowed assault training to continue satisfactorily, and from 31 August to 12 September a Regimental Combat Team (RCT) of the US 34th Division and a detachment from the US 1st Division trained at Inveraray followed by another 1st Division detachment between 14 and 26 September.

A further major difficulty for the 1st Brigade was the piecemeal arrival of its highly specialized equipment from the United States. All cargo manifests of ships arriving from the USA were scrutinized by staff officers, and detachments were placed at various ports to locate all Brigade equipment, which was then unloaded from fifty-five different ships arriving at six separate ports. With a great deal of hard work, the vital material was finally delivered to Rosneath for issue.

In September 1942 it was confirmed that Operation Torch would proceed as planned, with the 1st Brigade assigned to the Centre Task Force in the forthcoming invasion. All forces at Rosneath were now training intensively for Torch, along with the 531st Engineer Shore Regiment and units from the 286th Signal Company who had arrived from Northern Ireland. They formed combat teams and practised landing techniques at Rosneath, Toward and Inveraray. Elements of the 591st Boat Regiment from Northern Ireland went to Liverpool and to Immingham on the Humber where they learned the art of unloading ships' cargoes. A final concentrated effort was necessary to complete equipment needs and to acquire necessary additions, like bulldozers for beach clearance and steel mesh mats to overcome the hazard of soft sand on the beaches of north west Africa.

Some Rosneath peninsula residents had not been entirely happy about the new developments as large numbers of Americans arrived for a period of intensive training. The Kilcreggan Garage owner, Bryce Jardine, was certainly not amused when the first convoy of large, ten-wheeled US Army trucks, laden with troops, attempted to negotiate the tight turn at the garage forecourt where the narrow Portkil Lane joins the main Kilcreggan Road. As the leading truck, front fender adorned with sections of splintered fence, proceeded along the lane in the direction of the new rifle range, the young GIs, enjoying the situation, shouted in reply to the garage owner's irate remonstrations 'Never mind, Pop, we're gonna win the war for you. Send the bill to Uncle Sam'.

The difficulty of negotiating the corner without causing further damage to the garage forecourt and the proprietor's continued protest whenever further convoys of troop-laden trucks appeared convinced the drivers that further attempts to negotiate the tight turn were just not worth the hassle. Driving straight down off the main road, over the grass bank and onto the beach, they churned their way along the shingle towards the firing range.

The Farquhar family, who lived at Porkil, quite close to the range, were somewhat startled one summer day while enjoying a picnic lunch in their garden. They were rudely interrupted when a sudden and unexpected burst of fire from the direction of the range resulted in a hail of bullets whistling through the trees above their heads. The picnic was hurriedly abandoned, and from then on the family remained indoors whenever troops appeared.

By October 1942, strict security was the order of the day throughout the entire Clyde area. US Marines at Rosneath were authorised to set up sentry posts and to be prepared to use their firearms against anyone – including civilian contract workers – threatening the order or security of the Base. Meantime, the 39th RCT had arrived at Greenock with full combat equipment, vehicles, sixty days' supplies and ammunition. Following a short spell ashore, they joined a Clyde-based training exercise on 17 October. Units of the 34th Infantry Division also arrived in October to join the training programme. Loading of ships and full-scale landing rehearsals took place between 8-18 October, during which time a second RCT of the 1st Division practised landings at Rosneath and Toward. RCTs from Rosneath continued night assault landing rehearsals at Inverchaolain in Loch Striven while similar rehearsals took place around Inveraray. Combat Command 'B' of the 1st US Armored Division in Northern Ireland was likewise practising amphibious assault techniques.

Since 6 July, the British 1st Army, consisting of 5th Corps (4th and 78th Divisions), the 6th Armoured Division and the 22nd Anti Aircraft Artillery Brigade had been practising amphibious landing techniques in the West of Scotland. In early August, the 1st Army took part in a simulated beach landing exercise against opposition in Exercise Dryshod, which aroused doubts as to assault craft crew readiness to face real enemy opposition. As a result, it was decided that they should land in Algeria where only light resistance was expected. The British 11th and 36th Brigade Groups and two Commando units made up partly of US 34th Infantry volunteers would also take part in the forthcoming assault.

In mid-October, planning for Torch had been completed at Rosneath and the task force units were embarking for final training aboard the ships that would carry them to Africa. Assault convoy loading was directed by the British Army Movements Control, which caused some difficulties for the Americans who were unfamiliar with British methods. Faslane Military Port, and indeed all dock facilities in the Clyde area, worked to capacity as men and equipment were loaded aboard transports and troopships. Preparations for Torch involved some 440 special troop trains, 680 special freight trains and a total of 13,000 railway wagons as men and equipment were assembled on the Clyde.

By 17 October 1942, the ships of the Centre Task Force were at anchor in the Clyde Estuary within the protection of the Cloch/Dunoon boom defences. When joined by the Eastern Task

American troops board assault craft from Royal Navy ship off North African beach, 1942.

Force from Northern Ireland, they formed 'the mightiest assembly of shipping ever gathered together in any port in the world'. Residents of Gourock, Dunoon and the villages surrounding the upper Firth could barely see across the river because of the vast number of moored vessels. The assault ships of both Task Forces sailed for a final landing rehearsal just before daybreak on the 19th before returning to the Clyde to await their sailing instructions. All personnel were confined aboard ship, with very few exceptions, until 26 October, when both Eastern and Centre Task Forces – 274 transports and troop ships totalling 1,136,000 tons gross – left the Clyde under cover of darkness accompanied by a powerful naval escort.

US troops landing from small British assault craft in North Africa, near Oran, 1942.

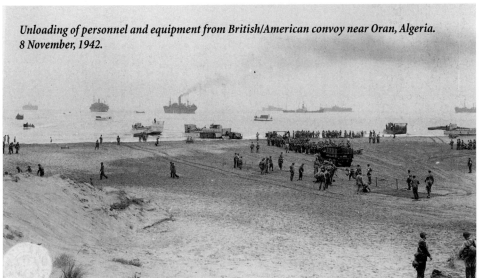

Unloading of personnel and equipment from British/American convoy near Oran, Algeria. 8 November, 1942.

US Soldiers in assault boats prior to landing on Algerian shores, 1942.

CHAPTER 5

SPECIAL FORCES

Rosneath and the Clyde area in general had been very busy during the preparations for Operation Torch. In addition to amphibious landing practice, extensive route-marching exercises had taken place around the lochside roads as columns of American troops foot-slogged from Rosneath to Arrochar and on to Inveraray. One day, Rab McMillan, the Birrell family's gardener at Stroul Lodge, Clynder, was perched somewhat unsteadily on a high ladder, hedge trimming by the main road, when he heard the sound of marching troops approaching but as yet out of sight around a nearby bend. Turning carefully to face the approaching column of soldiers, Rab, an ex-World War I veteran, came to attention as best he could given his precarious position and held his hedge knife in military salute as the American soldiers came into view. The lieutenant leading the first column smartly returned Rab's salute and ordered 'eyes left' to his men as they marched past. Rab had not realised that the group of soldiers was only the first of many, and each in turn received the 'eyes left' command from their lieutenant as they marched past the increasingly shaky gardener. Thankfully, when at long last the final column had passed, Rab climbed, stiffly, down from his uncomfortable perch.

Commandos, mainly from the Helensburgh area, also marched along the once quiet roads now perpetually busy with marching men, troop-laden trucks, halftracks, command cars, jeeps and various other military vehicles. The Commandos were billeted in Helensburgh along with US Army units who were receiving special training from the British. Patricia Drayton of Helensburgh recalls 'Yanks' being drilled in East King Street, between Charlotte Street and the public park. Girls working in the nearby Helensburgh Steam Laundry came outside at tea breaks to sit on a wall, watch the soldiers, make cheeky remarks and indulge in a little flirting.

Local man Jim Montgomery remembers two Commandos boarding with his family at Clynder in 1942. Each morning they departed to join their unit for training and returned in the evening with no indication of where they had been or what they had been doing. On a rare day off training duties, the Commandos stowed their equipment beneath their beds and disappeared. Jim and his brother, Jack, unable to resist a quick look, discovered, in great excitement, a machine-gun and other weapons.

The soldiers were from No.6 Commando who were training in the area at that time. After the disastrous Norwegian campaign in 1940, these units had been formed for future combined military operations and were stationed in western Scotland, sometimes living in tents or billeted with local families. The Commandos were independent of the usual military support services. Officers and men were issued with boarding allowances and instructed to find lodgings with local landladies.

On 22 April 1942, a letter in the *Helensburgh and Gareloch Times* expressed concern at the sight of commandos seen daily 'trudging around Helensburgh' seeking billets in private houses. The writer felt that the practice was demeaning for the soldiers, especially since a few householders rudely refused their request for lodgings. On 29 April, a Helensburgh lady who had four commandos billeted in her house wrote to express her concern at the attitude of some citizens to 'our brave fighting men' and expressed her belief that people 'must be sympathetic to them'.

Despite the off-hand treatment of these troops by some local householders, in early 1943, following the successful Allied invasion of North Africa, the local paper published a letter from Captain Donald Colquhoun of No. 6 Commando, younger son of Sir Ian Colquhoun of Luss, thanking the people of Helensburgh and district for the hospitality received when his unit was billeted in the area during training with the American forces at Rosneath. Captain Colquhoun added that 'the local landladies had become for the troops almost next to their parents'.

To offset the rigours of training and route marching, local people in general did everything possible to make their service guests welcome by providing entertainment for their off-duty hours. Popular weekly dances for servicemen and women were organised in Helensburgh and in the lochside village halls. Special fund-raising campaigns provided interest for the local population and military personnel alike and made a valuable contribution to the war effort.

US soldiers billeted in a Helensburgh home, 1942.

'Warship Week' in May 1942 included a grand parade in Helensburgh which was opened by Commodore Palmer, DSC, RN, with Lt Montgomery, USN, representing the Americans at Rosneath. A dance was held in Victoria Hall with a Royal Artillery band on stage while at Cove Burgh Hall a very successful social evening, organised by Miss M.L. Thomson, attracted over 100 guests, including locally serving members of the Allied Forces. At Faslane Military Port, in aid of Warship Week and by kind permission of the Commanding Officer, a boxing tournament was staged by the resident troops with an audience of soldiers and a number of invited civilian guests. Commodore Palmer and Lt Montgomery attended on behalf of their respective services. In addition to the recreational value of such events, Helensburgh and Garelochside, including Cove and Kilcreggan, raised the impressive total of £59,784 15s. 3d. for the national war effort, a substantial sum in the early 1940s.

On fortunately few occasions, the concentration of fighting men in the district produced unofficial boxing tournaments. On one Saturday night in May 1942, around 200 Faslane soldiers, locally stationed Commandos and local civilians fought a running battle along Sinclair and West Clyde Streets in Helensburgh. The problem had apparently originated in a minor incident at the Holyrood Dance Hall, known locally as the Honky Tonk, in James Street.

The dispute continued in the streets, leading to a general confrontation involving mainly soldiers but also some local civilians. 'Ugly scenes' developed as the police arrested ringleaders and crowds of combatants counter-attacked to free them. Several policemen were injured and several members of No. 6 Commando were arrested. One man was eventually jailed for sixty days and another fined the sum of £5 at the local court.

In June, a much happier Commando event was the dance held in the Victoria Hall in the presence of Commanding Officer McAlpine and his wife, who presented the prizes. On 1 July, an inter-Commando boxing match was staged in the Helensburgh Drill Hall, followed on the 29th by an exciting and well-attended display of realistic water manoeuvres given by Commandos at Helensburgh's swimming pool, including the ferrying of kit, supplies and weapons, by competing teams of military swimmers.

On 29 July 1942, the local press announced that 'men of a USN Task Force are now in Scotland operating with the Home Fleet'. On 5 August, the paper reported that when a Commando dance was held in Dumbarton, because of the temporary closure of Helensburgh's Victoria Hall, the 'Stars and Stripes' was suspended from the centre of the ceiling in honour of the American guests and that the event was 'a most enjoyable evening with a jolly cabaret show'. The *Helensburgh and Gareloch Times* revealed on September 2, that Helensburgh had experienced an American invasion when 'Doughboys visited shops to swap dollars for British coinage'. On the 9th, in 'Notes by the Way', a plea was made for 'something to be done to welcome hospitably our friends the Americans when in Helensburgh'. The article pointed out that the WVS canteen in the town was already strained by our own forces and that a haven of rest and recreation was needed for US soldiers to avoid:

> aimless wandering of the streets. The times are exceptional and the needs apparent. The Americans have come a long way from home to help us in our direst peril and it is up to us to reciprocate goodwill generously and spontaneously, and make their visit one to be recalled with pleasure.

The writer felt that the town council should tackle the problem but ended with the thought that 'with respect to the Town Council, it is slow to rise to an emergency'. A further letter, to the *Helensburgh and Gareloch Times* on 14 September 1942, again stressed the need for urgent action on the provision of forces' hostel facilities in the town as winter approached. A central site was needed but 'who will help ? The Town Council?' In fact, the YMCA had tackled the problem by acquiring Seacliff on East Clyde Street as a hostel for members of the Allied forces.

November saw the start of Sunday evening concerts in the Victoria Hall to augment the popular Saturday night Garrison Theatre evenings, both events being free to service personnel. On the 11th, the local press announced that Mrs Blythe's weekly dances for the troops featuring the Bill Breheny Dance Band were 'now in full swing' for the season, to the great delight of all, including the American guests. At the opening event of the new season, Lt Roy Stratton, USN, Rosneath Base supply officer, 'kindly volunteered' as pianist during the supper interval and proved to be such a fine player that 'keen dancers preferred leaving supper to others, and continue dancing'. Lt Stratton ended the evening by thanking Mrs Blythe for inviting members of the US Forces, 'which was greatly appreciated'. The twice-weekly dances in the Victoria Hall were very popular and as the local paper noted on 18 November 1942, 'on Thursday and Friday last' there was 'an excellent turnout of the services, chiefly men of the USN'. The Woodend Camp Regimental Band was on stage and 'many were denied entrance as the hall was full'.

Richard C. Key of Fresno, California, was one of many Americans who arrived at Rosneath in 1942, having already experienced the hazards of war as an armed guard radioman on the infamous PQ17 convoy to Russia. He enjoyed the local hospitality at Rosneath while training for Operation Torch.

Sam Maresca, from Williston, New York, a chief stevedore with the 5th Major Port Unit, US Army, was also at Rosneath in 1942. His unit was engaged in the handling of ships' cargoes at the Base and around the Clyde Estuary ports, on occasions loading vessels for the Murmansk run. Initially, the soldiers received their orders direct from London and worked on their own initiative since there were no officers with them at the time. When officers did eventually arrive to take charge, the enlisted men had to explain what was required, then train the officers in the art of cargo handling.

H.A. Singleton, USN, of Albequerque, New Mexico, landed at Gourock from the British troopship *Orion* and spent a week or two at Rosneath before being posted to Falmouth in southern England where his unit established and operated 'one of the best repair bases there was'. H.A. Singleton remained at Falmouth until 1945 when he returned home aboard the troopship *Queen Mary*.

D.J. Gavine, USN, from Enfield, Connecticut, came over in September 1942 aboard *Queen Elizabeth* and served at Rosneath as storekeeper third class, then acting chief until 1945. He enjoyed his time in Scotland and indeed met and married a girl while at Rosneath Base.

James Tsepas, USN, from Massachusetts, arrived at Rosneath in early October 1942, spending two years as a member of 'ship's company' until October 1944. James remembers his 'many happy days at Rosneath and in Scotland'. In 1943, he too married a girl whom he met while she was serving in the WRNS at Greenock.

Petty Officer Theodore ('Ted') L. Humes, USN, was typical of the many thousands of young American servicemen who, quite suddenly, found themselves at Rosneath in summer 1942, far from home and family. Ted had enlisted in May, and by early June was in Newport, Rhode Island, on a six-week basic training course. He was then posted to Pier 92, New York City, with the newly formed USN Amphibious Force. Pier 92 was an infamous naval shore station where regular navymen harrassed the newcomers and generally made their lives miserable. The only redeeming feature of the New York experience was the proximity of the famous and glamourous Times Square and the enjoyment of visits there during the warm evenings. Such pleasures soon ended when the young navymen were marched aboard the British ship *Reina Del Pacifico*, bound for Halifax, Nova Scotia, to join a convoy heading for Britain. Some two days out of Halifax a dramatic and tragic incident occurred when two US destroyers collided and one sank with the loss of all but seven of her crew. The apprehensive passengers on *Reina Del*

Theodore L. Humes, USN amphibious forces training at Rosneath, 1942.

Pacifico were convinced that the destroyer had been torpedoed. The rest of the voyage was uneventful, however, apart from boredom and the awful food dished up by the ship's catering department. It was so bad that Ted survived the voyage mainly on a diet of toffee and was relieved when the ship finally docked in Liverpool.

After disembarking, the company of three hundred or so marched from the dockside to Lime Street railway station where they had their first taste of warm English stout. Later that night they travelled by train to Helensburgh where they marched to the pier and the waiting landing craft that ferried them to Rosneath. Petty Officer Humes was assigned to a Quonset hut situated close to Rosneath House, USNAF Headquarters.

Ted remembers the area as a magnificent place to be situated and 'happily, we were spared the customary rain which I believe is typical of that area in the Fall'. After allocation of quarters, the new arrivals mustered in Division formation in groups according to their respective duties and were inspected by their Commanding Officer, Captain Spellman. The men of Rosneath Base were a varied group of specialists: medical staff, storekeepers, electricians, engineers, welders, and radiomen, indeed, all the skills required to operate and maintain a substantial, self-contained naval base. When Captain Spellman reached the catering staff of cooks and bakers he remarked, 'Ah, the most important of all'.

Ted enjoyed his time in Scotland. The weather was generally good. Captain Spellman's observation on the catering department was accurate and the men ate well. Shore leave was adequate and Ted has pleasant memories of his first time off-duty in late August, when, along with other 'liberty' men, he was ferried by landing craft to Helensburgh Pier. He also remembers being invited to a party at someone's home in Helensburgh where he was introduced to Scottish fish and chips. His hosts made him very welcome, and the girls present were 'first-rate'.

Many of the Rosneath Americans on leave travelled to Glasgow where they could stay in the American Red Cross Club in the city centre near Charing Cross. The Locarno Dance Hall in Sauchiehall Street was also a mecca for the Americans and for other service people visiting the city, and Ted has happy memories of his visits there. Even today the song 'Jealousy', a very popular wartime dance tune, brings back nostalgic memories whenever he hears it played. Many friendships were made; indeed Ted's best friend married a girl of the Women's Auxiliary Air Force (WAAF) whom they met at the Locarno.

Rosneath volunteers provided hospitality and a welcome haven at the Achnashie Canteen. Tea, sandwiches and home baking were constantly available. Lonely service people could just drop in for a quiet chat, a cup of tea, time to read or to write to the folks back home. One evening a group of US navymen, including Petty Officer Humes, were 'milling around' the canteen entrance in the gathering dusk, hesitantly shy of entering for the first time. Ted will never forget the moment when a kind woman, sensing their shyness, appeared at the door and said, 'Will ye no come away in?' They accepted her invitation, thoroughly enjoyed their evening, made friends and tasted British tea for the first time, served with milk, rather than American style, with sugar only.

All beds taken but the lounge at least is warm. Typical weekend for US servicemen on leave in Glasgow. American Red Cross Club, Charing Cross, Glasgow, 1943.

During a weekend leave at the American Red Cross Club in Glasgow, Ted had pinned a card on the club billboard just in case his merchant seaman brother, Henry, might visit the Clyde. A few days before leaving Rosneath, Ted was astounded to receive a telephone call from brother Henry, whose ship had indeed docked in Glasgow. Purely by chance, Henry visited the Club and was amazed to read his brother's note. A meeting was arranged and the brothers had a happy reunion before continuing on their separate wartime ways, which for Ted, as a member of the USNAF, led to embarkation on the transport ship *Neuw Zeeland* and the invasion of North Africa.

Ted Humes landed at Arzeu in Algeria where British Combined Operations Pilotage officers of the RNVR aboard HM submarine *Ursula* had carried out periscope reconnaissance of the beaches in the days preceding the Allied assault. During the early morning hours of darkness on 7 November 1942, *Ursula* surfaced to launch a canoe with two COP officers aboard who would anchor just offshore to signal in the approaching landing craft. Other canoeists of the British Combined Operations Special Boat Service had already carried out the hazardous task of landing senior US officers, including General Mark Clark, from a submarine at night on the North African coast for discussions with Vichy French leaders sympathetic to the Allied cause.

In Operation Kingpin, General Giraud and his staff were evacuated from southern France to aid the Allies in North Africa. Suspicious of British intentions, Giraud would only agree to leave if collected by a US submarine. Since no US boat was available, HMS *Seraph,* with a SBS canoe team aboard and a USN officer in nominal command was sent from Gibraltar by HMS *Maidstone.* When Giraud reached *Seraph* in the SBS canoe, he was quickly ushered below as the boat dived. On the following night HMS *Sybil* cautiously approached the French coast to pick up the General's staff. After an anxious wait close inshore a small boat approached the submarine whose commanding officer, Lt E.J.D. Turner, DSO DSC, a Helensburgh man, was surprised to hear a female voice softly through the darkness, 'They seek him here, they seek him there, those Frenchies seek him everywhere. Is he in Heaven? Is he in Hell? That damned elusive Pimpernel.'

The woman was the English wife of a French officer and when leaving the submarine she thanked Lt Turner, adding that she 'had returned to help carry the torch to victory'. The lieutenant was subsequently known among his fellow officers by the nickname Pimpernel.

CHAPTER 6

ROSNEATH SUBMARINES 1942-43

In August 1942, Prime Minister Winston Churchill had asked President Roosevelt for American submarines to help the Royal Navy and Royal Canadian Navy in their fight against the German U-boat threat. Submarine Squadron 50, commanded by Captain Norman S. Ives, was duly dispatched for duties in the eastern North Atlantic. The new submarines were Gato-class boats of 1,825/2,400 tons, with a maximum surface speed of around twenty knots, armed with ten torpedo tubes and two five- inch guns. In late October, the submarine tender USS *Beaver* arrived at Rosneath to await the arrival of the squadron's submarines.

The new boats, designed for long-range patrol in the Pacific Ocean, were big and well equipped, with a complement of nine officers and seventy-one enlisted men. Their presence in the Eastern Atlantic released the smaller British submarines for action in the relatively shallow

USS Beaver *and two Squadron 50 submarines at Rosneath, 1943.*

Mediterranean. Meantime, Squadron 50's orders had been amended, and the submarines proceeded initially to North Africa to support the Western Task Force of Operation Torch at Casablanca and Dakar. The Squadron, USS *Shad* (Lt Cmdr McGregor), USS *Gunnel* (Lt Cmdr McCain), USS *Barb* (Lt Cdr Waterman), USS *Herring* (Lt Cmdr Johnson) and USS *Blackfish* (Lt Cmdr Davidson) carried out pre-invasion beach reconnaissance and acted as beacons for the incoming assault craft of the Western Task Force. When these duties ended, Squadron 50's boats were ordered seawards to commence offensive patrols against enemy shipping. *Herring* sank a Vichy ship of some 5,000 tons while *Blackfish* torpedoed a vessel in convoy, being in turn attacked by enemy escort ships which forced her to dive deep to make good her escape.

On 14 November, Squadron 50's boats proceeded to Rosneath where they were re-assigned to patrolling the Bay of Biscay. *Gunnel* developed gear-train problems while heading for Rosneath and then all four engines failed. Lt Cmdr McCain radioed for help and, using the boat's Winton auxiliary, or 'dinkey', engine, headed slowly north until intercepted by a British rescue vessel that escorted *Gunnel* to Falmouth for repair.

USS *Gurnard's* departure from the United States was delayed by mechanical faults similar to those of *Gunnel*. She then proceeded directly to Rosneath and operated in European waters under the jurisdiction of the Royal Navy. Her engine problems continued, however, and she returned to the United States for major repair.

The other boats of Squadron 50 were powered by reliable Fairbanks-Morse or General

Action stations.

Motors/Winton engines as distinct from the new and relatively untested engines that had failed. *Herring*, in company with *Barb*, took over the Biscay patrols.

Blackfish sank a German vessel but was attacked by an enemy escort ship which damaged the conning tower forcing her return to Rosneath for repair. In April 1943, Squadron 50's submarines began joint patrols with British boats in the Denmark Strait. *Haddo* and *Hake* had arrived at Rosneath to replace *Gunnel* and *Gurnard*. *Barb*, HMS *Stubborn* and HMS *Severn* sailed from the Clyde on the 1st followed by *Blackfish* on the 5th. The US boats *Barb*, *Blackfish*, *Herring* and *Shad* shared these patrols with the British boats *Satyr*, *Surf* and *Truculent* until they were abandoned on 15 May and replaced by operations to the north and west of the Shetlands.

By June 1943, the United States Navy had concluded that Squadron 50 would be more gainfully employed in the Pacific Ocean and, with USS *Beaver*, they were ordered home for re-assignment. Prior to the Squadron's departure from Rosneath in 1943, their commander, Captain Norman Ives, received a message from Rear Admiral C.B. Barry, RN, Admiral of Submarines, acknowledging Squadron 50's valuable contribution to Allied operations during 1942-43:

> Without them it would not have been possible to have staged operations in anything like the scale we have. It is pure bad luck that they have not achieved more successes, especially so in the case of USS *Shad* who carried out one of the most outstanding attacks that has come to my notice. The targets that have come your way in European waters have been disappointingly few, but your submarines have invariably seized their opportunity and exploited themselves to the utmost. Their actual contribution has been very great and personal, far beyond the numbers of ships sunk or damaged.

To offset the discomforts of service aboard submarines, where conditions at sea were crowded, noisy, damp, smelly, unpleasant, often tedious and always dangerous, American boats were noted for their excellent food. To compensate further for the pressures of war patrol, special facilities for the Rosneath submariners were organised at the village of Drymen, near Loch Lomond. The USN took over the Buchanan Arms Hotel as a 'Rest and Recreation' centre where crews could relax between patrols. When Squadron 50 left Rosneath in 1943, the Buchanan Arms R&R facility was taken over by the 8th United States Army Air Force (USAAF). A US Army Signals Unit stationed near the Botanic Gardens on Glasgow's Great Western Road organised accommodation and travel arrangements for the airmen. Exhausted USAAF bomber crews from southern airfields were dispatched to Drymen for well-earned rest periods before returning to the dangers of daylight bombing raids over Germany. Dances and outings were organised for the airmen, and bicycles could be hired for leisurely trips around the peaceful and picturesque countryside.

Captain Norman Ives did not return to the United States with Squadron 50 in 1943 because of his appointment as Commanding Officer at Base Two, where preparations had begun for the next step in the Allied plan: the invasion of France.

CHAPTER 7

NEXT STEP OVERLORD

Following the successful invasion of North Africa in late 1942, the US Navy had no immediate need of Base Two apart from the continued presence of Squadron 50 and its maintenance force. With some reservations, they handed the base over to British control in early 1943, retaining sections of dock, workshops and accommodation required for Squadron 50 submarine operations and the Seabees at Clachan House 'K' section. Recommissioned by the Royal Navy as HMS *Rosneath*, the Base continued to operate as an Amphibious Operations Training Establishment under the direction of Rear Admiral H.T. Baillie-Grohman, RN, Combined Operations, Naval Headquarters, Largs.

After the departure of the Allied forces training for Torch in 1942, the Gareloch district experienced something of a breathing space. Following the German defeat in North Africa, however, preparations for the invasion of France began and military activity on Garelochside rose again.

View of British section of pier at Base Two, 1943.

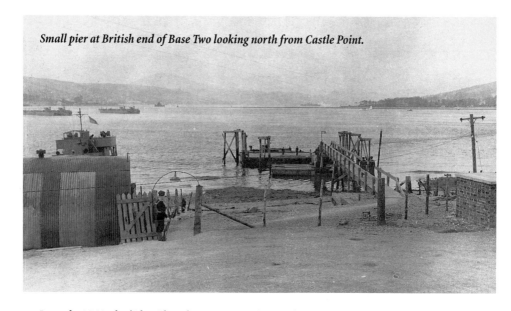

Small pier at British end of Base Two looking north from Castle Point.

In early 1943, the 'Rhu Church War Entertainment' group appealed for public donations of cakes, tea, sandwiches and cigarettes in order to continue organising local events for the forces. They reported that during the past year they had disbursed some 3,200 free teas and over 1,000 free cigarettes to visiting service men and women. The weekly dances for service men and women in Helensburgh, organised by the redoubtable Mrs Blythe and her helpers, continued with their usual capacity numbers. On 23 June, Lt Col W. McClure D.S.O. T.D. held a party at Ardtarman House. Invited guests included Pioneer Corps officers and many Allied representatives, including 'old friends from the Norwegian and American navies'. The Pioneer Corps orchestra supplied 'the most enjoyable music' for the occasion.

During a 'Wings for Victory' fund-raising campaign in early summer 1943, Mrs Maxwell of Cove, secured the services of a company of distinguished artistes, led by Sir Harry Lauder, who appeared at a grand concert in Cove Burgh Hall with the RAF orchestra supplying the music. In June, US Navy officers from Rosneath held a dance and show attended by over 200 guests, including civilians from Helensburgh district and officers from the various military units in the area. Music was provided by the Double Two Pioneer Corps Dance Band from Faslane Military Port, and the local newspaper correspondent wrote that 'the show was lovely' and the catering 'excellent'. The paper also reported that on 16 June there was a large attendance at a National Fire Service dance in Cove Burgh Hall, with music by the Erik Maxwell Dance Orchestra.

In more serious vein, the *Helensburgh and Gareloch Times* of 7 April 1943 contained a letter from General Dwight D. Eisenhower, Commanding Officer, Allied Forces in North West Africa in which he wrote:

> The British Commandos' superior work when attached to the assault force at
> Algiers merits special commendation. Prior to embarkation, detachments of US
> officers and men were attached to a Commando unit for training. The outstanding

leadership of their Lt Col and the spirit of comradeship shown by the officers and men of the Commando won the unqualified loyalty and admiration of the GIs. The training and experience received by those Americans under such leadership have made them an invaluable asset to future training in the US Army.

In April, the authorities announced the introduction of 'coastal restrictions', which the public saw as a broad hint of an impending invasion of Europe. The main Scottish river estuaries would be regulated and civilian access restricted in certain areas where security was paramount because of military training or other activities relating to the forthcoming landings in France. In the Clyde Estuary, this order applied between Ardrossan and Glasgow where areas designated as high security would be closed to unauthorised civilians. Gareloch district had effectively been under such security controls for some time, with civilian access restricted by the military at Faslane Port and at Rosneath. Plans were well under way for Operation Overlord, the top secret amphibious assault on France, and the provision of accommodation, training and supplies for large numbers of American troops in Britain was now a matter of the highest priority.

Rosneath's potential was again recognised by the US Naval authorities on 20 August, 1943, when, on the orders of Commander, USN Forces in Europe, the Base was returned to American control and recommissioned as USN Base Two, Main Receiving Station for USN activities in Europe. It would serve also as a training, supply and maintenance base.

On 1 September 1943, Base Two was transferred from USN Forces in Europe control to that of Landing Craft and Bases Europe, with Rear-Admiral John Wilkes in command. From August 1943, the base was continuously busy as the American naval forces prepared for the invasion of France. Rosneath Bay, the dock areas and nearby beaches were in constant use as ships and landing craft arrived and personnel received amphibious assault training. Ships of the Gunfire Support Group of the US Navy's Eleventh Amphibious Forces, crewed by 1,900 men and four assault troop units totalling 5,750 men, trained at and around Base Two and in the sea lochs of the Clyde Estuary. Rosneath's facilities were used to the fullest possible extent at this time as the Amphibious Force's fleet of artillery and rocket firing ships and assault craft prepared for combat.

In November, Captain Norman Ives relinquished command of Rosneath and was replaced by Commander E.S. Stoker. Captain Ives now assumed responsibility for the training of the special navy construction battalions (DREW Units) which would be required for clearing captured beaches and ports and setting up bases in France. DREW Units 1, 2 and 3, consisting of some 1,500 officers and men, were training at Rosneath during this period; indeed, all DREW units bound for Normandy trained at Rosneath following their arrival from the United States.

In July 1943, men of the 29th Seabees were transferred from Rosneath to build the new amphibious assault bases in the south of England.

Civilian pass to travel main loch side road at Faslane Military Port.

British LCT on beach, Camsail Bay near Rosneath House and facing Rosneath Base industrial area, 1942

At Rosneath, preparations for the invasion of France continued. On 10 October 1943, Submarine Chasers 683 and 718 arrived from the United States, followed on the 15th by SC 1061. On the 26th, all three vessels were transferred from the USN to the US Office of Strategic Services which handed over command of the ships to the Royal Norwegian Navy. With Lt L. Hauge of the RNN in command and manned by Norwegian naval crews, the three vessels sailed from Rosneath bound for Scalloway, Shetland, The crews were mostly former Norwegian fishermen, and the arrival of the submarine chasers at Rosneath was the result of a search for suitable vessels to replace the slow and vulnerable fishing boats used to maintain links between Shetland and undercover operations in occupied Norway.

When Admiral Stark, Commander in Chief of American naval forces in Europe, heard of the search he requested the dispatch of three sub-chasers from the USA and in the words of Lt Cmdr David Howarth, RNVR, in *The Shetland Bus*:

> The whole weighty efficiency of the American Navy came to our aid and everything
> happened with bewildering speed. Within a week things were moving in Florida.
> Three submarine chasers were loaded on merchant ships. Within three weeks of
> the first request they arrived at various ports in this country and assembled in the
> Clyde. We knew nothing about their capabilities, except that Admiral Stark said
> they were just the thing for the job. I went down to the American base at Rosneath
> and awaited their arrival with the utmost interest. When I saw them coming into
> the Gareloch, looking like young destroyers, I was as excited as a schoolboy.

Following a week of instruction by the American sub-chaser crews, the Norwegians set off up the west coast bound for Scalloway with one American officer and three engineers aboard to advise in the event of any problems arising during the passage. In fact, the boats, as Admiral Stark had said, proved ideal for the job.

When Rosneath Base returned to American control in 1943, personnel numbers increased, and in the month of November 1943 rose by nearly 100 per cent over the preceding month. This increase put a severe strain on local recreational facilities, and the Achnashie Club at Stroul was no longer able to cope with such numbers. The problem had been recognised by the Women's Voluntary Service (WVS) management in October 1943, when they officially assumed responsibility for Achnashie Canteen and realised that its services had to be improved. A sum of £1,100 was allocated for a new modern building and, with the addition of local donations and fund-raising events, local yacht designer James McGruer was commissioned to prepare plans for a new building and to supervise its construction. On 8 August 1944, the new canteen was officially opened with due ceremony. Commander Pamperin, USN, and Mrs Cornock of the American Red Cross were present, along with other locally stationed service representatives and village dignitaries.

To augment Base leisure facilities, Clynder Hotel was requisitioned, with the exception of the public bar area. The building became an American Red Cross (ARC) Club where enlisted men could escape from service life for an evening and enjoy dancing with invited local girls to the latest American music played by the base dance band. The adjoining public bar section was declared out of bounds to USN personnel, senior officers occasionally looking in to check that the ban was being observed. During one inspection, an officer found a group of enlisted men drinking at the bar and ordered them to leave. The bar proprietor unwisely intervened to argue on their behalf, but he was wearing a USN jacket acquired from a previous off-limits naval customer and was immediately told to remove the garment forthwith and hand it over. The chastened bar-owner was warned that if caught again wearing navy clothing he would be reported to the local police and charged with theft.

Captain L. Sabin Jr, USN, arrived to assume command of the Gunship Support Group of the Eleventh Amphibious Forces on 11 December 1943. The month continued with increasing numbers of fully laden landing craft and freighters arriving from the United States with cargoes of DREW unit materials and equipment. All departments worked to capacity as they dealt with newly arrived assault craft and large quantities of ammunition for storage in the Base's magazines. Personnel numbers reached a new peak in December, with some 4,000 men and 275 officers permanently quartered in addition to the many arriving from America and awaiting transfer to ships and shore stations throughout the UK.

The first three months of 1944 were increasingly hectic at Base Two as the Allied build-up for the cross-channel assault gathered momentum. Numerous Landing Ship Tank (LST) and Landing Craft Tank (LCT) arrived from the USA laden with materials and smaller landing craft. Following maintenance checks, refuelling and taking on fresh stores, they were dispatched south to the various US Navy amphibious bases. By 14 February, personnel numbers had reached the record total of 6,329 and when Landing Craft Flak (LCF) 31 was taken to the Lamont Castle Shipyard at Port Glasgow for repair, this indicated perhaps that Rosneath's capacity was overstretched. Two US Army Craft Harbor Companies were at Rosneath during the period from March 1944, the 333rd with forty-four vessels and 221 officers and men and the 345th with six craft and 62 crew.

An unusual event took place on March 13 when twelve members of Landing Craft Vehicle and Personnel (LCVP) crews from the Gunfire Support Group, Eleventh Amphibious Assault

Force, were decorated for outstanding performance of duty during the invasion of Italy. The awards were presented at Rosneath by the Base commander, 'with appropriate ceremony at Meritorious mast'. Margaret Saunders of Helensburgh was employed at Rosneath House, USN Headquarters, and watched the ceremony from a window overlooking the parade ground. She had been sent to work at Rosneath by the Helensburgh Employment Office. Initially, she was unhappy at the prospect of the tedious daily return bus journey to Rosneath and did not want to work at the base. When she had settled in to her new job, she realised that her fears had been ill-founded. Working conditions were good and her Rosneath days were happy and well paid, with excellent and generous meals provided free of charge. These included fresh fruit and chocolate, rare treats for civilians in 1944.

The Americans were informal and friendly, regardless of rank, and Margaret remembers sitting with the other girls on upturned buckets in the cleaners' cupboard enjoying coffee and a smoke during rest breaks. Occasionally, an officer joined them in the den where he too would perch on a bucket with coffee and a cigarette in hand to enjoy the conversation.

A less pleasant memory for Margaret is her recollection of the day when she and fellow worker Grace Jardine heard loud shouting in a foreign language. A group of men wearing German uniforms suddenly burst into the building, rounded up all personnel at gunpoint and marched them outside, explaining in English that they had landed in Scotland to capture USN headquarters. The girls were frightened, in tears and concerned for their safety, wondering who would inform their families of their fate. As they were being marched out with the others, the

LST loading troops and equipment in preparation for D-Day 1944.

girls managed to slip into a side room unobserved, opened a window, escaped from the building and ran for their lives. Breathless, they came upon a lone American who listened to their tearful story then consoled them with the reassurance that it was only a security exercise. He convinced the girls that the mock attack had been staged to impress on headquarters personnel that they must be prepared for any emergency. He then escorted the girls back to Rosneath House.

Inspection visits by senior USN officers were a regular diversion at Base Two. On 14 March, Rear-Admiral J.J. Broshek and Captain Chapline of the Bureau of Ships arrived, followed on the 27th by Rear-Admiral G.B. Wilson and Commodore C.C. Baughman. On the 23rd, the repair ship USS *Melville* had arrived to assist the hard-pressed Base personnel with the LST rearmament programme for the invasion of France. Several LST were dispatched to Londonderry for urgently needed materials. The closing days of March 1944 were very busy, as four LST docked while eleven arrived to load cargoes for Milford Haven. The month ended with the arrival of a Dutch merchantman to load materials for the 111th Seabee Battalion in the south.

During April and May 1944, the pattern of activity continued with a constant flow of men and supplies arriving from the USA in the final buildup to the impending invasion. HMS *Marie* berthed to discharge cargo. Two LST arrived with materials, and a seemingly endless number of fully laden LST sailed from the Gareloch, bound for Brixham, Falmouth, Dartmouth and Appledore. USS *Melville* continued with the LST rearmament programme while ships arrived regularly from the United States with military supplies. Torpedo boats and coast guard cutters arrived to await orders, and minesweepers came alongside to load sweeping gear. USS *Melville*, having completed her duties at Rosneath, sailed on 1 May for Portland in Dorset, and by the end of May a decline in numbers at Rosneath was evident as personnel were deployed south in readiness for the invasion.

The memorable month of June 1944 began unusually quietly at Base Two. There was a marked reduction in the number of ship movements. On the 2nd, seven motor torpedo boats, along with USS *Summers* and USS *Davis,* arrived to take aboard fuel and supplies before sailing on the 3rd. SS *Whitestable* sailed on 6 June, D-DAY, for the invasion of France.

The first lift of DREW 1 personnel and equipment from Rosneath Base to France took place on 13 June, following the initial success of the landings in Normandy and the urgent need to clear available French ports. DREW 2 personnel and materials followed on the 16th aboard USS *Achernar,* while USS *Miantinomah* and USS *Christian Flanagan* docked at Rosneath to load more DREW unit equipment for France.

During this anxious period as the Allied armies fought ferociously to extend their grip on Normandy, Base Two's normal routine continued, but the first real evidence of the Normandy conflict at Rosneath was the arrival of wounded American survivors. In all, some three thousand were received, given necessary medical attention at Portkil Hospital, issued with new clothing and allocated quarters. All Base facilities were at the disposal of these men while they recovered from their ordeal and awaited reassignment in the UK or repatriation to the USA.

Raymond Drake of Beverly Hill, Florida, a machinist's mate with DREW 5, had boarded the troopship *Queen Mary* at Pier 92, New York, in January 1944 and arrived in the Clyde some five days later. Together with the other DREW units already at Rosneath, they spent their days training in preparation for port-clearing duties in France. Raymond clearly remembers the

USS Ancon, command ship assault force 'O', during D-Day landing at Omaha Beach, June 1944.

US landing craft of the initial attack head for Omaha Beach, D-Day.

Landing craft approaching Omaha Beach. Smoke on shore from naval guns in support of troops, D-Day.

Assault troops carrying equipment on Omaha Beach with amphibious and half-track vehicles, D-Day.

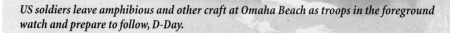

US soldiers leave amphibious and other craft at Omaha Beach as troops in the foreground watch and prepare to follow, D-Day.

tremendous amount of naval activity in the Firth of Clyde at that time: the battleship USS *Texas*, the cruiser USS *Tuscaloosa* and the 'great armada of Allied aircraft carriers and many other naval vessels'. Machinist's Mate Drake and DREW 5 remained at Rosneath when the other DREW Units left for southern England and the invasion of Normandy. DREW 5 remained at Base Two until July, when they took a train from Helensburgh to Plymouth and sailed for Cherbourg aboard USS *Miantinomah*.

William K. Walters of Boston, Massachussets, was with a supply detachment of DREW 1 when he left New York in January 1944 aboard *Queen Mary,* 'along with 20,000 other service people it seemed'. Quartered seven decks below sea level, they received two meals daily, but the 'chow' lines were so long that after queuing in the crowded passageways many just didn't much care if they ate or not. Bill fell ill with a chest infection and was sent to sick bay where he was issued with sulpha tablets but with only enough water from a communal cup to swallow one pill. Throats were treated with a communal swab and 'what you didn't have before you were confined there, you soon developed'. Bill's infection led to pneumonia, and he was very glad when they reached Scotland and he was transferred to Portkil Hospital at Rosneath Base until fit for duty.

Bill Walters' mother, a Kirkpatrick from Ulster, had had a brother living in Scotland until his death in 1909. After settling in at Rosneath, Bill wrote to 'any Kirkpatrick at his uncle's old address in Prestonpans'. Incredibly, his eldest cousin's sister-in-law was the local district postmistress and the letter was duly delivered to this cousin who asked Bill to visit the family in Musselburgh. With some leave due, Bill set off from Rosneath. While waiting for a bus in Edinburgh he met a Scot who insisted on paying his fare since, as a merchant seaman, the Scot had been so well treated in America that he felt honour-bound to repay such kindness. At Musselburgh, Bill asked the bus conductor's help for directions and he in turn asked a passenger if she could assist the visitor. On learning that Bill sought the Kirkpatrick house, the woman exclaimed, 'You'll be their American cousin'. Bill was the first ever US Navyman to visit the town, and he spent Easter weekend with his Scottish family. Neighbours generously contributed their precious food rations in order that the Kirkpatricks could fittingly entertain their guest.

Bill finally left Rosneath with DREW 1 aboard a Navy transport ship in June, shortly after D-Day, bound for Cherbourg. Because its harbour was so heavily mined and blocked with sunken vessels, however, Bill's ship remained at sea for 'such an extended time that she put into Milford Haven, Wales, where the men were taken ashore for a seven-mile hike'. It was hay making season and Bill, to this day, 'can still smell the fragrance of that new-mown hay'.

Richard R. Morrissey Jr of Fresno, California, served with DREW 6 Amphibious Group at Fowey in southern England and in October 1944, shortly after his eighteenth birthday, found himself in Rosneath along with another 1,500 or so DREW personnel. Assigned to the carpenter's shop on maintenance duties, Richard had his own flatbed truck to get around the various jobs and vividly remembers the first day when he had to leave the Base and drive on the highway. He was startled when he realised that his vehicle was on the wrong side of the road but quickly pulled over before becoming involved with other traffic. He also remembers many LST at Rosneath dock awaiting transfer to the Russian Navy and being impressed by the ceremony and the sight of Russian officers in uniform. Another memory is that of his first glimpse of a contingent of Dutch marines stationed at the Base and their 'colorful powder-blue uniforms'.

Richard also recollects being taken with a work party to 'near Garelochhead', where they were 'engaged in shifting and loading depth charges, hard work and a little touchy'.

Base Two personnel were obliged to use the official naval ferry from Rosneath to Helensburgh, but Richard and others sometimes 'used to cheat a little' by taking the civilian ferry from Kilcreggan to Gourock and the train to Glasgow, 'which was a lot easier than fighting the crowds to Helensburgh and grabbing fish and chips before beating someone to the train. We were not supposed to go that way but got away with it most times'. Richard and his friend often visited the Locarno ballroom in Glasgow and 'wound up with some nice girlfriends named Gow and Urquhart and met their families'. During his time at Fowey, Richard had met Ruth Gowan and in 1944 he travelled by train to St Blazey, near Fowey, to spend Christmas leave with the Gowan family. He and Ruth were serious about each other but, as with so many wartime romances, they drifted apart and eventually lost touch.

Chief Petty Officer Arthur Gallagher and his wife Jean, the author's sister.

Chief Petty Officer Poplin and mascot.

Rosneath Base officers.

Rosneath baseball team.

CHAPTER 8

THE PACE SLACKENS

The success of the Normandy landings was followed by a gradual rundown of USN bases in the United Kingdom. At the end of June 1944, LST medical crews, no longer needed in Europe, left Rosneath for transfer to the Pacific. A marked decline in dock activity was evident, and nearly 1,000 officers and men left for the United States in July of whom 720 had been attached to the repair ship USS *Milwaukee*. On 5 August, however, two new groups arrived – 1,232 officers and men of DREW 4 and 1,147 of the 114th Seabees to participate in a new training course.

An unprecedented event at Rosneath occurred on 7 August, when a party of legal officers led by Lt Commander Steinberg, USNR, arrived to hold General Courts Martial of two enlisted men: the first charged with theft and absence without leave, the other accused of murdering two marines. The Court decided to recess while awaiting a medical report on the latter, whereupon it

Picnic party, Rosneath.

reconvened and continued, with Lt J. Perkins acting as Judge Advocate and Lt Cmdr Steinberg as President of the Court. Proceedings were completed by 24 September. The Base War Diary does not reveal the Court's findings.

On 24 August, Captain Sadilec, US Army, and his contingent of 160 men and four officers responsible for armed guard duties at Rosneath were replaced by USN personnel who took over security duties. During August, as Allied military success in Europe continued, increasing numbers of US Naval personnel arrived at Base Two from bases in England and Normandy for shipment home, leave and reassignment. On the other hand, some 2,500 officers and men arrived from the USA of whom half joined DREW 4 unit training at Rosneath, the balance being posted to other USN bases and naval craft requiring crew. The decline in activities at Rosneath continued during the latter months of 1944. Only two ship movements took place and the daily courier service to USN Headquarters in London ended on 15 September. Nearly 1,400 personnel left for the USA, including 88 from Base Two 'ship's company'. On 19 September, however, Captain H.R. Holcombe, Commanding Officer of DREW 4 and his staff of forty officers and 160 men arrived for Base duties. On 28 September, Admiral Sir Richard Hill, RN, inspected Rosneath, accompanied by Commander Pamperin, USN. Numbers at Rosneath had dropped substantially. Only twenty-five men arrived from the United States although some 2,000 officers and men were temporarily resident while awaiting shipment home.

In October, thirty-three men of Base Two 'ship's company' left for home along with 1,500 officers and men from other USN bases, but 62 officers and 634 men of DREW 4 arrived from southern England on the 19th. A mere ten men arrived from the US for assignment, of whom seven went to Iceland and three remained at Rosneath until posted to a base in England. This was a new low in personnel assignments, and the Rosneath Base was at its quietest since the arrival of the civilian construction force in the summer of 1941.

Perhaps because of the lull in military activity at Rosneath, in November 1944, the occasion arose for a demonstration of other USN talents. The Base choir, consisting of twenty-six officers and men organised by Chaplain R.E. Ellington and conducted by Lt Karl A.B. Petersen, sang in Rosneath Church to a large and appreciative audience with solos by Seamen Clifford Ross, J.E. Robbins and J.T. Conroy. The popular choir also received an enthusiastic welcome at other venues, St Andrews Church, Helensburgh, and the Usher Hall and St Giles Church, in Edinburgh.

The improved national security in the UK as the Allied armies continued their advance in Europe was evident in November 1944 when the Home Guard was 'stood down'. The pause at Rosneath was temporary, however, as the month continued with an upturn in activity beginning on the 11th, when SS *Charles Wilson Peale* came alongside to load cargo. On 13 November, Pier 2 was damaged as the perhaps aptly named LST HMS *Bruiser* attempted to come alongside. Two complete piles and some twenty feet of curb beams required replacing by the Base Seabees. Another official visit occurred on the 13th, this time by Lt Cmdr J. Hillensuis of the Royal Netherlands Navy regarding the possibility of training Dutch marines at Rosneath. On 15 November, Pier 4 was damaged when US LST 331 experienced difficulty while docking. On this occasion no new piles were required but a Seabee crew spent a week on repairs. Two more LST docked without incident on the 15th to await decommissioning by the US Navy and Lend-Lease transfer to the Royal Navy.

This was a new departure at Rosneath and the first of many such transfers of American craft to the British Admiralty as the US Navy concentrated its attention on the Pacific War and disposed of equipment now surplus to its needs in European waters. On 18 November, 139 Dutch marines arrived for a training course, the first of several contingents to undergo training at Base Two, and on the 20th, Lt Cmdr Reeser arrived as commanding officer of Dutch personnel at the Base. During the remainder of the month, no fewer than nine American LST were officially handed over to the Royal Navy.

December began with yet another visit by a high-ranking group, Rear-Admiral L.E.H. Maund, C.B.E., RN, and party, who inspected facilities at Rosneath. The transfer of US LST to the Royal Navy continued, seven in all during the month. A new administrative task for Base Two staff also began in December when twenty USN patrol torpedo boats berthed for Lend-Lease transfer to the Russian Navy. Captain Schrader, USN, was appointed acting commander of Task Forces 124 and 126 which were being assembled at Rosneath for training as future administrators in postwar Germany, while Draft Nine of the 69th Seabees reported for temporary duty of some six weeks' duration to prepare 'F' Area of Base accommodation for the new training forces.

A few days later, two Soviet Navy officers, Captain P. Koslov and Lt Captain Bondaruik arrived at Rosneath. They were responsible for checking the condition of Lend-Lease vessels being transferred by the American authorities to the Soviet Navy, and, most unusually for senior naval staff, they donned overalls and closely probed every corner of each vessel, including the most inaccessible bilge sections. The Russians confided to an American officer that if a Lend-Lease vessel arrived in Russia with any corrosion, they would pay the price, each drawing a finger significantly across his throat. As Russian sailors arrived to crew the Lend-Lease vessels, all American facilities for welfare and recreation at Rosneath were put at their disposal.

On 23 December, for an officially undisclosed reason, US seaman guards and Petty Officers received orders to carry arms and were stationed in all vital areas of the Base. Extra security measures were to be taken that would remain in force until further notice. The remaining days of December saw the arrival of sub-chasers for shipment back to the USA, a number of LST with cargo and miscellaneous US assault craft for transfer to the Royal Navy.

During the month of December, some 1,500 officers and men, including the crews of decommissioned ships and some from other stations in the UK, were received and shipped home. None came from the USA however, but RN personnel arrived to crew ex-American landing craft, and numbers increased to the extent that a new RN canteen was established at the Base.

January, February and March 1945 were months of continuing activity at Rosneath as the new European Affairs Division (EAD) was set up to train personnel for the immediate postwar administration of Germany. Maintenance teams at the Base's industrial section were also busy as they prepared craft for transfer to the Russians. During this period, three Landing Craft Mechanised (LCM) and nine LCVP arrived for duty with EAD activities at Base Two as a result of a Base inspection on 22 November, 1944, by Vice-Admiral Glassford, USN. The Admiral's visit had resulted in a lengthy memorandum to Admiral Stark at USN headquarters in London regarding problems at Rosneath. The main concern was the 'grave morale problem' among the temporary personnel training at Base Two for future occupation duties in Germany. The causes of the problem were attributed to 'inadequate leadership, boring academic lectures, a lack of recreation facilities, an indifferent local population, too few dances, insufficient feminine companions and the isolated situation of the Base'. The officers and men of the occupation training forces were additionally disheartened by the long-drawn-out state of the war in Europe. They were impatient with the seemingly endless training and the feeling that they had been forgotten and would never see real action as the Navy's role declined. The constant transfer of personnel to and from various tasks throughout the UK destroyed unit pride and discipline, and many men complained of inadequate indoor sports facilities, a lack of 'movie shows' and a poorly stocked Ship's Store.

On 12 February 1945, a memo from Captain Schrader, Commander of Training Force 124 at Rosneath, commented on the alleged morale problem and pointed out that Base Two had been considered for closure since June 1944. Consequently, the Base had received only make-shift repairs until November when the official decision to train the 'occupation forces' had resulted in the release of sorely needed maintenance materials. In answer to the allegation that Rosneath personnel, including officers, were slovenly of dress, the memo pointed out that Base Two had been built in 1941 when the possibility of air-raids was very real. Facilities had been deliberately dispersed over a wide area for sound defensive reasons, making transportation within the Base a problem, and the 'perpetual damp raw climate' made personnel smartness hard to achieve. Hooded parkas and galoshes were essential when men often had to walk in the rain on muddy roads, especially after working hours. The inclement weather and winter darkness made outside sports often impossible, and off-duty personnel faced the problem of a shortage of suitable ferry craft which made access to Helensburgh difficult. In bad weather even the existing liberty boats were unable to operate, and men returning to the Base would find themselves stranded in Helensburgh or facing a fifteen mile hike around the Gareloch, often on dark, windy and wet nights. On these occasions groups of men stranded in Helensburgh would club together and stop a passing car or truck, offering the driver cash to deliver them to Rosneath.

The Doughnut Dugout run by the American Red Cross at the former Clynder Hotel was outside the Base perimeter and a visit involved acquiring an off-Base pass and a lengthy walk, not always attractive after a day's work, particularly on a rainy evening. Suggested solutions to the problems of going off Base, either to the local Red Cross or farther afield, included the possibility of moving the local ARC Club to a site within the Base perimeter and the opening of another ARC Club in Helensburgh with 50 to 150 beds available for men stranded 'ashore' during bad weather. Meanwhile, it was agreed that on occasions when the liberty craft were storm-bound, stranded personnel would be collected from Helensburgh by bus.

By March 1945 Captain Schrader had examined the problems of low morale and his report indicated some remedial success. The ferry service to Helensburgh was now much better and various improvements had been made to recreational facilities. These included more dances with invited female guests, students from Glasgow University who were transported to and from Rosneath by special bus, more frequent programmes of recent Hollywood films and improved audience facilities with more efficient heating to offset the damp cold of a Scottish evening. British ENSA concert parties had visited Rosneath but were not very popular with American audiences who preferred their own USO shows. Navymen also organised concerts, using Base

The Bob Hope Concert Party with Frances Langford and Jerry Colona.

personnel talents and on occasions local musicians. Boxing matches were promoted at the Seabee camp near Rosneath village to which locals were invited, and on a notable morale boosting occasion in 1945, Base Two received a visit from the very popular Bob Hope Show with Frances Langford, Tony Romano and company. The author, a teenager at the time, was taken to the concert by a group of navy friends, and Harry Turner of Kilcreggan, another local teenager in 1945, also attended the show with navy friends and accompanied them to a post-show party at the Princess Louise officers' club where he met the stars and obtained their autographs which he treasures still.

Regardless of reported problems of boredom and lack of entertainment opportunities among the more recently arrived and temporary personnel of the EAD, the Base Seabee maintenance crews, medical staff at Portkil and other members of the regular 'ship's company' had, contrary to Admiral Glassford's comment about 'local indifference', established local friendships and were warmly welcomed into many family homes. In appreciation, the Americans repaid such hospitality by providing their hosts with food, chocolate, cigarettes or cigars, strictly rationed in Britain but readily available to navymen in the Base commissariat. Many families in the peninsula's villages and farther afield welcomed lonely Americans and other service visitors into their houses where they could relax and briefly escape from military surroundings. Long-standing friendships were made, and despite the passing of the years, some have survived and the occasional American veteran still returns to visit and remember.

Stuart Edwin Fraser, USN (retired), wrote to the *Helensburgh Advertiser* in 1975 of his days at Portkil Hospital as a medical corpsman. Boarding the troopship *Queen Mary* at Pier 92, New York, on 15 August 1942 with the first draft of hospitalmen bound for Rosneath, he arrived at Gourock five days later. The unit was then ferried to Rosneath and quartered in huts surrounding the 200 bed hospital at Portkil. Stuart spent two years there and remembers his stay as being 'very happy'. During weekend 'liberty', he and his friends would travel to Gourock by ferry then by train or bus to Glasgow. They also enjoyed dances at Cove Burgh Hall and at the Cragburn in Gourock where everyone was 'very friendly'. Stuart married an Edinburgh girl, and two of his fellow medical corpsmen likewise married Scottish girls, Hugh Sang a girl from Glasgow and Walter Jinks a Gourock girl.

Local newspaper articles by Patricia Drayton of Helensburgh describe the days when GIs from Rosneath trained at Helensburgh with British Commando instructors. She confirms the friendliness and good-natured generosity of the Yanks as they handed out candy, gum and other goodies to all and sundry. Many local residents were very grateful for food, particularly fresh fruit and 'cigarettes and cigars which the Americans seemed to have in plenty'. Patricia also recalls her wartime schooldays at Hermitage School and the occasion when a group of Americans from Rosneath were invited to join the platform party at the school Christmas service. After the ceremony each girl was delighted to receive a box of American chocolates but there was nothing for the boys. Rosneath peninsula children were particularly favoured because of their proximity to the Base and received frequent invitations to parties. Some locals still have pleasant memories of these events at Portkil Hospital, Clachan Camp or at Rosneath House headquarters, where they were well fed and entertained.

The Rutherford family of Rosneath were one of many local families who established enduring friendships with American navymen, and on one occasion, when exercising their dog in the woodlands surrounding their home, they were attracted to a particular holly tree by the dog's furious barking at someone in the branches above. A closer look revealed a somewhat embarrassed officer gathering berried holly. On descent, he apologised profusely, explaining that he was the Base Episcopalian padre seeking holly with which to decorate his church hut for

Ted Humes visits Rosneath 1997, fifty five years on from 1942.

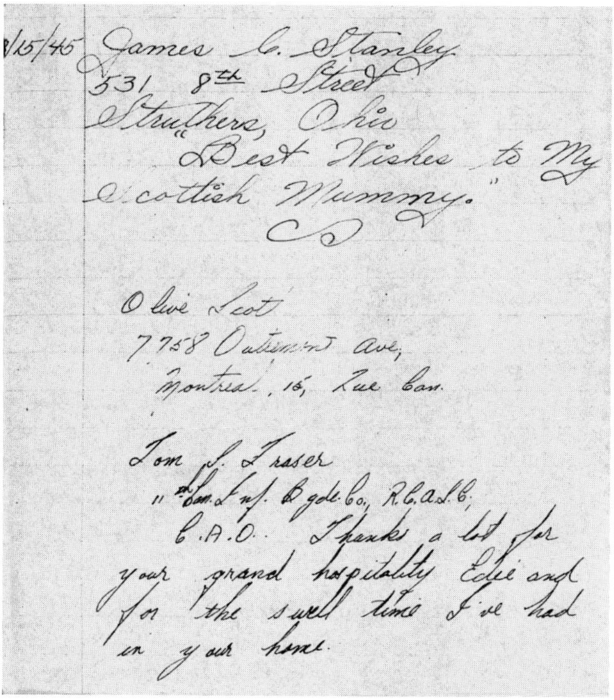

Pages from the Birrell family visitor's book.

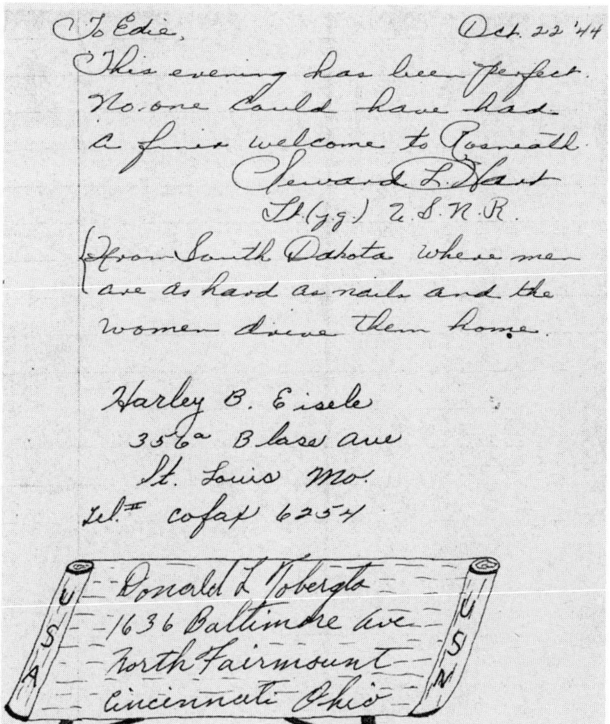

1/15/45 James C. Stanley
531 8th Street
Struthers, Ohio
"Best Wishes to My
Scottish Mummy."

Olive Scot
7758 Outremont Ave,
Montreal. 15, Que Can.

Tom J. Fraser
11th Can. Inf. Bgde Co. R.C.a.S.C.
C.A.O. Thanks a lot for
your grand hospitality Edie and
for the swell time I've had
in your home.

To Edie,   Oct. 22 '44
This evening has been perfect.
No one could have had
a finer welcome to Rosneath.
Seward L. Hart
Lt(jg) U.S.N.R.
From South Dakota where men
are as hard as nails and the
women drive them home.

Harley B. Eisele
356a Blass ave
St. Louis Mo.
Tel# cofax 6254

Donald L Toberto
1636 Baltimore ave
North Fairmount
Cincinnati Ohio

Christmas. He had not realised that he was on private woodland and gratefully accepted the offer of all the holly he needed and a drink at Kilarden, the nearby Rutherford home. The padre and the Rutherfords became firm friends who kept in touch regularly over many years.

At Stroul Lodge in Clynder, the Birrell household was another of the many village homes where a warm welcome was extended to American and other servicemen who were always free to spend off-duty hours as members of the family. On returning to their own homes and loved ones when the war was over, they carried with them many fond memories of Bob and Edie Birrell, their daughters, Margaret and Helena, and the generous hospitality at Stroul Lodge.

The working day at Rosneath Base allowed little time for boredom. The Base supply department in particular was fully occupied at this time, providing ex-American sub-chasers with provisions, fuel and ammunition in preparation for their voyage to Soviet waters. The maintenance Seabee units were equally hard-pressed maintaining Base equipment and repairing the numerous vessels moored alongside. In January, a group of six naval gun-crew survivors had arrived at the Base, followed by another group of twenty-six in March and three groups totalling twenty-seven in April. Their ships had been lost by enemy action and the survivors were given temporary accommodation at the Base while awaiting repatriation.

Meanwhile, the Rosneath routine continued as boats of USN Patrol Torpedo Squadrons 34 and 35 arrived to be decommissioned and prepared for transfer to the Russian Navy. The redeployment of personnel continued however as 151 enlisted men and eight officers left for the United States. On 28 April, Engineer Rear Admiral Brykin, head of the Soviet Naval Mission in London, arrived with a party of his staff to inspect the latest batch of twenty-four sub-chasers transferred to the Soviet Navy and about to depart for Russia.

Although the remainder of Draft 9 of the 69th Seabees left in April, six officers and 230 men of Section 1, Detachment A, 30th Special Seabees, arrived for duty with Headquarters Company Task Force 12. As April ended and the daily routine at Rosneath Base continued, the war in Europe, despite fierce enemy resistance, headed inexorably towards the final German collapse. As the end approached, the US Navy prepared to close bases, reduce European operations and concentrate their naval forces on the defeat of Japan.

CHAPTER 9

THE FINAL STEPS

Rosneath received a significant visit on 20 April 1945 when Rear Admiral H.E. Horan, RN, Chief of Combined Operations Bases (Western Approaches), accompanied by senior and junior staff officers, carried out a detailed inspection of Base facilities. On 26 April, another senior visitor, Lt Admiral Furstner, arrived to inspect the Dutch marines training at Rosneath. Shipping movements continued as surplus equipment was loaded for return to the United States. American assault craft arrived for decommissioning before transfer to the RN, and the level of activity at the Base rose again as the four-year-long presence of the US forces entered its final stage. On 4 May, thirty-nine men and one officer of Draft 8, 97th Seabees, departed for Heathfield in England. On the 5th, another significant day for Rosneath, a dispatch arrived from Commander, US Amphibious Bases in the UK, announcing that 15 June 1945, was the target date for the end of the US Navy's tenure at Rosneath.

The war in Europe was virtually over and the official announcement of unconditional surrender by Germany had been expected on Monday 7 May, 1945. The surrender documents were signed in the early hours of Monday and the British people, including King George VI, prepared to celebrate immediately. The Allied governments, however, jointly announced the official time of VE Day as midnight Tuesday, 8 May. At Rosneath the villagers and their American friends had prepared a huge bonfire in a field near Clachan House. Despite the official announcement, the Rosneath fire was lit after dark on Monday night. Technically, blackout restrictions remained in force and the village policeman arrived to insist that the blaze be extinguished forthwith. By this time, however, the bonfire, fuelled by Lend-Lease kerosene generously supplied by Seabees from their nearby Clachan Camp, was beyond normal control. The village constable called out the US Navy fire-fighting force, but as water began flowing on to the flames, the revellers counter-attacked with bayonets and other assorted instruments, piercing the hoses and causing a series of fountains that soaked one and all and reduced the water flow to a trickle. At this point, officialdom decided to retreat, and amidst cheers from the happy throng, the local lawman and naval firefighters surrendered the field.

DREW Units 4 and 6 and Headquarters Company Task Force 126, a total of 831 men and 70 officers, left Rosneath on 6 May, led by Captain Harold R. Holcombe. On the 8th, US Torpedo Boats 554 and 560, along with LCT 1163 and LCT 1176, were handed over to the Soviet Navy. Also on the 8th, US Twelfth Fleet amphibious craft were decommissioned at Rosneath, their crews leaving for Plymouth to await transport home. Twenty-five men, the balance of the Base armed guard pool, left on the 14th for Cardiff, and a further 79 personnel followed on the 16th, the last of DREW Units 4 and 6.

The end was near on 17 May, when a party of seven RN officers, led by Commander Hindley-Smith, arrived for duty in advance of the transfer of Rosneath Base to the British Admiralty. On the 19th, 226 personnel, the balance of Combined Task Force 126, along with 243 from the 30th Special Seabee Battalion, left Rosneath for shipment home and subsequent relocation to the Pacific. On the 20th, however, nine officers arrived from Plymouth and Exeter to advise on and assist with the final disposition of the remaining materials and equipment before Base Two was finally handed over to British control. A group of 250 moved out on 31 May, bound for Southampton and home, including 149 from Base Two 'ship's company' and 92 from the 97th Seabee, Base maintenance force. This was the first large departure of regular Rosneath personnel preceeding the imminent American handover.

Shortly before leaving for home, after some four years of close co-operation with the Royal Navy, a final and somewhat ironic official duty for a small party of American officers was their visit to Kirkbean, in southwest Scotland, birthplace of John Paul Jones. With the approval of Admiral Stark, C in C, US Naval Forces in Europe, they presented a specially carved stone font to Kirkbean church in memory of John Paul Jones, the Scottish seaman who had settled in Virginia and who in 1775 'hoisted the first American flag as sanctioned by the Congress of the United States aboard the thirty-gun ship *Alfred*'. The infant United States Navy carried the American struggle for independence to British coastal waters in 1777 when Commander Jones in USS *Ranger*, and again in 1779 as commodore of a small French squadron, flying his flag aboard *Bon-Homme Richard*, challenged British seapower in a series of daring engagements with ships of the Royal Navy.

The month of May 1945 was again a busy period for the US personnel remaining at Rosneath, especially for those of the Supply Department who were responsible for disposing of all remaining stores and materials. Fifteen US Army trucks and twenty-three loaned by the RAF helped the Base Two truck fleet deliver the bulk of the goods to nearby Faslane Port where they were loaded on to railway wagons for delivery to the USN Supply Base at Exeter. The remaining small stores, spares, provisions and miscellaneous supplies were taken directly by road from Rosneath to the USAAF Transport Command at Prestwick airfield. Dutch marines quartered at Rosneath Base provided work parties to help the Seabees and other American personnel remaining at Base Two. Work proceeded on a twenty-four hour routine to comply with the deadline of 15 June.

*The last dance at Princess
Louise Officers' Club.*

U.S. NAVAL COMMUNICATIONS

INCOMING MESSAGE

CLASSIFICATION : **CONFIDENTIAL**   DATE : **14 JUNE 1945**

FROM :	ACTION :
COMPHIBSUKAY	**COMINCH CNO**

TIME RECEIVED : **1530B**

DECODED BY : _____

WRITE UP BY : **HOPE**

PRECEDENCE : **DEFERRED**

INFO : **COMNAVEU, COMPHIBSUKAY, DIST. LST I, II, III & V, NSD BAYONNE, ADMIRALTY, SHAEF, ANCXF, CINC, WESTERN APPROACHES, CINC, PLYMOUTH, CINC, PORTSMOUTH, FOIC GREENOCK, RACOB(W.A.), HMS WESTCLIFFE, S OF I, GREENOCK, S OF L, ROSYTH, SCE, GLASGOW, EEM, ROSYTH.**

130849B

U. S. NAVAL BASE TWO, ROSENEATH, SCOTLAND, DECOMMISSIONED AS OF 0800 13 JUNE 1945. REQUEST ALL BUREAUS AND OFFICES BE ADVISED.

CO'S FILE	SPDC—2—
COMM FILE	PWMC
PERSONNEL	MED. STOREHOUSE
DISBURSING	DISPENSARY
TRANSPORTATION—2—	30TH C.B.
RMO	97TH C.B.—2—
RPIO	1049TH C.B.
SUPPLY—2—	

CR#1325

Following the handover, small groups of Americans remained at Rosneath to instruct incoming British personnel in the use and maintenance of American equipment. On 1 June 1945, the final entry in Base Two's War Diary was dispatched to Washington by Commander A.T. Pamperin, and on 14 June, the United States Navy officially announced that Base Two, Rosneath, Scotland, had been decommissioned at 08.00, 13 June 1945.

During the eventful years of close partnership between British and American naval forces in World War II, some 124,000 officers and men of the United States Navy, including 11,350 Seabees, had served in Europe. Base Two's contribution was pivotal to the success of Allied amphibious operations in North Africa, and although far from the bases in southwest England that played the major role in the final preparations for D-Day, Rosneath was of great logistical importance in supporting and supplying these bases. Among the great variety of ships and craft that were repaired, rearmed or re-supplied from Base Two during the months of hectic D-Day preparation were those of the US Navy's Transport Divisions 1, 3 and 5, the battleship USS *Texas*, USS *Arkansas*, USS *Tuscaloosa*, USS *Nitro*, USS *Mount Baker*, two torpedo boat flotillas, a US Coastguard rescue flotilla and a flotilla of LST.

Clachan House area, July 1945, now the site of Rosneath school.

Rosneath House, July 1945.

THE POSTWAR YEARS

In June 1945, Base Two reverted to British control as HMS *Rosneath*. A variety of assault ships and other craft filled the harbour awaiting Admiralty decisions as to their future. With the final victory over Japan in August, Rosneath and Garelochside returned to peacetime conditions, but with reservations. The postwar world was fraught with new international tensions, and national defence remained an important priority. Rosneath Base continued as a Combined Operations establishment, and in 1947 a proposal to update its amphibious training facilities was considered. The American dock would be rebuilt and the tank farm retained, along with all buildings and facilities of the main industrial area and 'K' section accommodation at Clachan

South end of dockyard at HMS Rosneath, *July 1945. Shipping and landing craft await decisions as to their future.*

Postwar reserve fleet battleship in the Gareloch.

Postwar reserve fleet carriers at Rhu.

House. A new jetty and barracks area for Royal Marine Commandos was planned for the area adjoining the tank farm in early 1948, but these proposals were abandoned. Rosneath Base was closed and eventually dismantled to make way for a new school and church, new housing and a section reserved for small industrial developments. Little evidence remains of the wartime US Base with the exception of two now dilapidated oil tanks, and several rusting sheds, one of which has recently been refurbished for use as a motor repair shop.

After 1945, the Gareloch gradually filled with surplus ships, many destined for Metal Industries Ltd, the new ship-breaking enterprise established at the former Faslane Military Port in August 1946. The Royal Navy used the southern section of Faslane wharf for de-storing ships prior to laying them up in the loch as units of the Reserve Fleet.

In December 1946, the *Helensburgh and Gareloch Times* reported that the crews of the submarines HMS *Vulpine* and HMS *Virulent*, 'at present in reserve in the Gareloch', held an enjoyable Christmas party in Helensburgh's Holyrood ballroom. The newspaper also reported a sad naval accident when a rating from the Gareloch Stoker's Training Establishment fell overboard from a tender lying alongside Faslane jetty. Despite a brave rescue attempt by a colleague who dived into the icy water, the unfortunate man perished.

British/American naval co-operation continued after 1945 as the Cold War years of confrontation between Russia and the West gave rise to the North Atlantic Treaty Organisation in 1949 and the later British/American agreement to site a US nuclear submarine force in the Holy Loch. Joint naval exercises took place regularly, and between 13-17 September 1957, eighty British and American warships gathered in the Clyde Estuary before sailing for exercises in Eastern Atlantic waters. USS *Cadmus*, a submarine repair ship, joined 'units of the Royal Navy and the United States Navy including . . . nine submarines' which would take part in the 'forthcoming exercises'. *Cadmus* proceeded upriver to Faslane on 17 September, where she remained until the 30th as submarine emergency depot/repair ship for the duration of the combined exercises. *Cadmus* occupied the berth recently vacated by HMS *Jupiter* following the transfer of Reserve Fleet headquarters to Rosyth. On the 24th, it had been announced that HMS *Adamant* and the Third Submarine Squadron would move to Faslane from Rothesay Bay after the exercises, but *Adamant's* arrival was delayed due to illness among her crew, a press report revealing that 'after . . . an outbreak of Asian flu . . . she is due back on October 14 to take up . . . permanent station in the Gareloch'.

Shortly after the units of the Third Submarine Squadron arrived at Faslane in 1957, they received a top security visit from USS *Nautilus*, the world's first nuclear-powered submarine. In 1962, at the Nassau Conference, the United States agreed to provide technical assistance to Britain and to sell Polaris missile systems to the Royal Navy. At the opening of the RN Polaris School at Faslane Base in 1966, Vice-Admiral H.S. Mackenzie referred in his speech to the 'closest co-operation between the Americans and ourselves', a situation continued in the present agreement whereby the Royal Navy's latest boats are armed with American Trident missiles carrying British warheads.

This close association between the two navies remains visibly evident today. Submarines of the United States Navy regularly visit Faslane almost sixty years since the special and unique relationship was established during World War II when the United States Navy built the Gareloch's first operational naval base at Rosneath.

US nuclear boat in the Gareloch, 1999.

opposite:
HM Naval Base, Faslane, 1999.

Derelict USN oil tanks at Rosneath, 1999.

USN shed at Rosneath, 1999, now a car repair shop.

INDEX